T0095590

You Are Today's
WOMEN
OF THE
BIBLE
and I Can Prove It

I am a Child of God,
and I Am Woman

DARCI JEFFRIES

ARCHWAY
PUBLISHING

This book is a work of non-fiction. Unless otherwise noted, the author and the publisher make no explicit guarantees as to the accuracy of the information contained in this book and in some cases, names of people and places have been altered to protect their privacy.

Archway Publishing books may be ordered through booksellers or by contacting:

Archway Publishing
1663 Liberty Drive
Bloomington, IN 47403
www.archwaypublishing.com
1 (888) 242-5904

Because of the dynamic nature of the Internet, any web addresses or links contained in this book may have changed since publication and may no longer be valid. The views expressed in this work are solely those of the author and do not necessarily reflect the views of the publisher, and the publisher hereby disclaims any responsibility for them.

Any people depicted in stock imagery provided by Getty Images are models, and such images are being used for illustrative purposes only. Certain stock imagery © Getty Images.

ISBN: 978-1-4808-5969-2 (sc)
ISBN: 978-1-4808-5970-8 (hc)
ISBN: 978-1-4808-5971-5 (e)

Library of Congress Control Number: 2018903379

Print information available on the last page.

Archway Publishing rev. date: 03/23/2018

Commit your works to the Lord
And your plans will succeed

—Proverbs 16:3 (NLT)

I dedicate this book to my heavenly Father and to those involved in getting this book out to you. There are so many. I am sure that if I listed them, in my senility, I would forget someone. My sons and my grandsons have influenced me tremendously. But most of all I have written this book for my daughters-in-law and beyond a shadow of a doubt for my granddaughter, my granddaughter-in-law, and the women my grandsons will be adding to the family along the way. If even one woman reads this book and acts on what her Lord is asking her to do, it will all be worth it. This book is dedicated to all the women whom God has asked to step up or out who are hesitating for whatever reason. Hopefully, this book is just what the doctor ordered. (Once a nurse, always a nurse.)

Contents

Introduction

Why does anyone write a book? There's an itch to scratch, a bone to pick, or a voice to be heard. And anyone with a tight relationship with God knows what a nag He can be if He wants you to do something, particularly if you're not obeying. Besides, my drawer where I started saving papers before computers were around is getting full. Now that computers are here, saving things is easier. But they're still a group of who-remembers-what and when-will-you-do-something-with-them space on my screen.

To my amazement, one day all the things in my drawers and on my computer started to come together in my head. I heard God say, "It's time." I had made a few attempts at writing a book before, but nothing seemed to work out well, and I had no desire to follow through. This time things were different. Not only were the words coming together, but things were also dropping in my lap that pertained to this book. I would read something in a daily devotional or hear a sermon, and God would say that I needed to put that in this part of my book. People who could help me with whatever I needed at the time showed up in my life even if they were someone I'd never met before.

As I fell asleep one night, the title of this book came to me, as well as how to write about women in the Bible and tie them in to what is happening to today's women of God. It struck me that if God were going to write the Bible two years from now, who would He put in it? Us! It would be each one of us, even if we are not walking with God right now.

My hope is to get women to understand how important we are to God's kingdom work and to God. We need to see that we, today, are doing the work that Mary Magdalene, Deborah, and Esther did in the Bible. We are not better than men, but we are as instrumental as men in God's workplace. And maybe we wouldn't respond as Jael did (drove a tent spike into the enemy soldier's head using a hammer) physically, but metaphorically, why not?

I hope that you enjoy reading this as much as I enjoyed writing this. God's blessings to you and yours.

BOOK 1

1

Been There—Was That!

I am a child of God, and I Am Woman.
This is not a women's lib book for women of the Bible.

So why write this book about women of the Bible that does not always make men look the best? The reason God has led me to write this book is to help both men and women to recognize the important roles women played in the Bible. Today, women still have important roles to play influencing people for God's kingdom. It is because of those women and the roles they played in biblical history that today's women, no matter what age, what level of education, what financial status, or whatever we use to measure ourselves against other women, still have that same level of influence as did the women of the Bible.

We are today's women of the Bible, and I can prove it.

The goal of this book is not necessarily to get more women in the boardroom but to get more women working with others for God's kingdom. "The harvest is plentiful, but the workers are few" (Matthew 9:37).

We should not compare ourselves to one another. God has made each of us individuals with our own callings or destinies. When we start to compare ourselves to others, jealousy can become a by-product of that comparison. But we do compare.

Marvin Williams, one of the authors who contributes to *Our Daily Bread*, wrote an article titled "Comparison Obsession." He wrote, "Comparison obsession isn't new. The Scriptures warn us of the dangers of comparing ourselves to others. When we do so, we become proud and look down on them (Luke 18:9–14). Or we become jealous and want to be like them or have what they have (James 4:1). We fail to focus on what God has given us to do. Jesus intimated that comparison obsession comes from believing that God is unfair and that He doesn't have a right to be more generous to others than He is to us (Mt 20:1–16)."

He continues, "By God's grace we can learn to overcome comparison obsession by focusing on the life God has given to us. As we take moments to thank God for everyday blessings, we change our thinking and begin to believe deep down that God is good."

You need to be you. Like teenagers, sometimes as adults, we want to blend in instead of standing out. If God wanted us to be the same, He would have created us as such. But He didn't do that. There is a job for each of us to do, a reason He put us here.

When speaking about people who work for God's kingdom, I include and laud those women who feel the Lord wants their ministry to be their husband, children, and maybe a neighbor or relative or two. Not all of us are to be a Joyce Meyer and speak before thousands. If we go outside our assigned fields, we will not be successful. Some mother had to raise Mother

Teresa. Some wife is standing strong behind her pastor husband who is positively affecting the thirty parishioners who make up their small church. And of those thirty parishioners will come ten missionaries who bring in hundreds of workers for God's kingdom. I would love to outlaw the statement, "I am *just* a housewife." When you are obeying God's direction in your life, you will be blessed while here on earth. When you get before God in heaven and need to account for your days on earth, He will honor you for your obedience. Never allow yourself or anyone else to put you down as just a housewife. You are an obedient servant of God and as such deserve respect. You are a housewife!

Here are examples of what "just" housewives can do.

Eunice and Lois: Mother and Grandmother to Timothy

Paul felt that he could trust Timothy with the responsibility of other Christians because of what Timothy was taught as a child (2 Timothy 1:5). His grandmother, Lois, and mother, Eunice, instilled faith in God in Timothy as a child, and that faith was still in Timothy's spirit when he became part of Paul's group of disciples. Timothy was instrumental for the growth of God's kingdom. Hurray for grandmothers!

As my grands are heading out into the world, the best thing I can do is pray, pray, pray. I want to keep them physically close but am so proud of the adults they have become working for our Lord's kingdom. While my heart hurts to not be able to cuddle them anymore, my spirit rejoices with pride to be able to share them with the world. Tears of mixed emotions are cathartic, helping me to release them to their callings and to God. For some reason, I find it harder to let go of my grands than my sons.

I like to think that we influence, or at least set in place, things that help our grandchildren to become who they are in Christ. I know for sure that a grandmother's prayers work.

As Psalm 71:18 says, "Now that I am old and gray, do not abandon me, O God. Let me proclaim your power to this new generation, your mighty miracles to all who come after me."

Jochebed: Mother of Moses, Aaron, and Miriam

These siblings were chosen to lead the Israelites out of bondage (Exodus 6:26; 15:20). Plus, Aaron later became the high priest, and his family continued to perform the duties of the priesthood. Miriam was also known as a poetess and musician and as involved in the Israelites' escape from Egypt as her brothers.

As a mother myself, I stand amazed at what Jochebed must have instilled in her children to have all three become who they were; all honored God. Jochebed could have been angry with God that Moses was taken from her as a baby. But she honored the fact that Moses appeared to her to be a gift from God. Jochebed is also known as one of the heroines of faith (Hebrews 11:23).

Jochebed went against the law of the Pharaoh, who gave the order that every newborn boy should be thrown into the Nile (Exodus 1:22). She saw something in Moses that made her want to chance the possibility of what would happen to her if she did not obey the law (Exodus 2:1–8).

But at one point, Jochebed had to let Moses go.

She created a waterproof basket and placed Moses in it. I can't imagine what she must have felt as she let that basket go into the river. It had to have crushed her heart.

Miriam ran along the riverbank to be sure that Moses was okay. He was discovered by Pharaoh's daughter. She felt sorry for the baby and decided to keep him. When a wet nurse—meaning a woman who could nurse a baby—was needed, Miriam volunteered to find one.

As Jochebed's reward for taking the chance to save Moses, the Lord worked it out that Jochebed could nurse her own son, even though he would grow up in the Pharaoh's family, not hers (Exodus 2:7–10). The chances we take for our children!

If you weren't being honored as a woman who gave birth to someone prominent, you were being honored as a woman who was the wife of someone prominent. Since we are talking about Moses, let's stay in his life for a moment longer.

I am impressed by what his wife did to keep Moses from being killed by God before he had a chance to lead the Israelites. You know what they say: behind every good man is a good woman. This was true for Moses. He would have died and not been able to lead the Israelites if she had not acted.

Zipporah: Wife of Moses Who Saved His Life

The name means little bird or sparrow. When Moses killed a man, he fled from Pharaoh and right into the arms of his wife (Exodus 2:15–22). He discovered her at the well drawing water for her father's flock. They had their first son and then another.

The burning bush was the way God decided to

communicate with Moses at that time. Perhaps God needed something dramatic to get Moses's attention? It took a bit of negotiating for God to convince Moses that he was the one to lead the Israelites out of Egypt (Exodus 3:10). After Moses learned of his assignment from God, he took his wife and sons and returned to Egypt (Exodus 4:20).

At a point in their travels, God showed up angry at Moses, possibly because Moses did not circumcise his sons. God was about to kill Moses (Exodus 4:24–26). So, Zipporah took out her flint knife and cut off both sons' foreskins and touched Moses's feet with it (Exodus 4:25–26). Since this is a quoted scripture, I can only make a few assumptions as to what "it" is referring to. With further research, I found that in Jesus's day, often one part of the body would be used to refer to an unmentionable part of the body. Therefore, my assumption is that Zipporah took the bloody knife and touched Moses's part of the body, his feet, that corresponded to his removed foreskin. The bottom line is that she saved Moses's life and put her sons in a better place to be right with the Lord. Way to go, Zipporah!

I can't even begin to imagine putting the words *flint knife, foreskin,* and *sons* in the same sentence. Performing the act would be nearly impossible for me, and I am a retired ICU/ER nurse who has seen and done a few things myself. Any men who are reading this, you can sit up straighter and uncross your legs now. No one is after your family jewels.

What an influence her family was to Moses. It was also her father who helped Moses to establish the first judicial system (Exodus 18:14–26). That's a lot of influence from a woman hardly noticed in the Bible.

She is not mentioned again after she and her sons are returned to Moses by her father following a time of separation.

Most of us don't remember her name unless we look it up. But then, I guess, the topic (the surgical procedure) makes this a Bible story that you wouldn't read at night to your children as you tuck them into bed.

Many women of the Bible are known only for the children they raised. God must have thought that important when He put together the Bible. Look anywhere in the Bible where a king is mentioned, and you will find out the name of his mother. There are only a few where the mother is not listed.

Mothers are often given credit for how well or poorly their children have turned out. Those of you who feel God is asking you to minister to your families could well be raising a king. Or by supporting your husband, you are allowing him to do something for the kingdom of God that he might not have been able to do without you!

Hezekiah was twenty-five years old when he became king, and he reigned in Jerusalem twenty-nine years. His mother's name was Abijah daughter of Zechariah. (2 Chronicles 29:1)

Jehoahaz was twenty-three years old when he became king, and he reigned in Jerusalem three months. His mother's name was Hamutal daughter of Jeremiah, she was from Libnah. (2 Kings 23:27)

There is an opposite situation with King David. David is included in sixty-six chapters in the Bible, yet his mother is basically unknown. His father and siblings are not only mentioned, but their names are given as well. Little is said about his mother.

However, King David does acknowledge her in

Psalm 86:16: "Turn to me and have mercy on me: show your strength in behalf of your servant; save me, because I serve you just as my mother did."

While she remains nameless in the Bible, it is hard to miss her influence in David's life. We see him succeed, we see him fail, but we also see the strength of God in his life. The power of a mother's influence is not always seen before the mother dies. Her influence is part of her children's life, long after she is gone and in the generations to come.

Her faith, her example, and her influence affect her grandchildren and beyond. It all positively transcends generations. Great-grandchildren who never meet their great-grandparents can also become godly men and women because of past influences. One of them may also become someone after God's own heart.

Dr. David Jeremiah, in his monthly devotional, *Turning Points*, wrote about President William McKinley's mother: "President William McKinley grew up in a devout Methodist home, and he was close to both his parents. His mother's faith was like an umbrella over his entire life, and her humble service for the Lord became a model he followed in public life."

Dr. Jeremiah goes on to say: "We never know how our influence for Christ will change the world. God calls us to love others by encouraging and building each other up. When we raise our families, serve our churches, and make peace in our neighborhoods for Christ's sake, we're letting God's love flow through us."

I saw a sign on a local church billboard that said, "A Mission Field Can Be Overseas or Over the Fence." You owe no one an explanation or excuse for being a stay-at-home missionary. Be at peace.

Another goal of this book is to help others to become

a friend of God's. Would you consider yourself a friend of His?

A friend is defined in Webster's Dictionary as: "A person whom one knows and with whom one has a bond of mutual affection, typically exclusive of sexual or family relations." Do you talk to God like you would your best friend? "Thanks for that parking place, God. Look at that woman who is wrestling with kids and grocery bags and waiting for the bus. Please help her, Lord. Thank You, Lord, for that perfect lampshade You helped me find today."

Scripture supports that God had some who were considered His friend. He also let us know what we need to do to become His friend.

Our God, did you not drive out the inhabitants of this land before your people Israel and give it forever to the descendants of your friend Abraham? (2 Chronicles 20:7)

But you, Israel, my servant, Jacob, whom I have chosen, you descendants of Abraham my friend. (Isaiah 41:8)

You are my friends if you do what I command. I no longer call you servants, because a servant does not know his master's business. Instead, I have called you friends, for everything that I learned from my Father I have made known to you. (John 15:14–15)

Many times, trying to become a friend of Jesus has all the right components, like prayer time and the desire to be closer to Jesus, but not faith in the relationship with God. Why would Jesus want to consider me His friend?

The Lord would speak face-to-face with Moses (Exodus 33:11). Before Jesus's resurrection, there was always someone between God and a human. That human was designated to be the mouthpiece for God.

But now, the veil has been torn, and we are face-to-face ourselves with our Lord. He is ready to be friends with any of us and all of us. We just must find a way to become that friend. More on this topic to come.

I love men. Really, I do.

Without men, women would have a completely different and very boring identity. We can establish our own individual image of who we are as a woman. But who we have become as a complete woman "ping-pongs" off the men in our lives no matter what role they play.

My Lord and my Christ are portrayed as men, and along with the Holy Spirit, I am passionately in love with each one of them. I raised two sons who have become godly husbands and fathers. I have five grandsons and one granddaughter who are presently walking with God in their lives. My sons have added to the woman I am as a mother. I ping-pong off my grandsons' identities because as their "Mimi," I have influenced them. Hopefully I have added to the men in Christ that each of them has become.

As a side note, I also love my granddaughter beyond words, but right now we are talking men in my life. And the Great Planner has blessed me with two daughters-in-law who are raising my grandchildren and loving my sons with the passionate love of Christ. A granddaughter-in-law, who is also passionate about God, has been added to the gang.

I have loved and lost a male soul mate—a man I lived with for fifteen years before I was saved. While I have lost a husband to divorce, I have gained true friendship in him and his wife. We have formed a nontraditional family that celebrates the holidays and our grands together. We socialize at times and have seen fruit from this relationship. We all three went to the same church for a long time. Others would come up to one of us and tell how our relationship has made them want to try harder with their ex.

I've had dear, dear male friends depart from my life through death of one form or another. Some have left through a physical death, others by death of a friendship. The fact that two male family members decided to sexually abuse me is a large part of what has made me the woman in Christ I am today. Because of that abusive experience, I have ping-ponged my way through counseling, healing, and triumph. I have moved from victim to victor. And I have matured from needing help to being that help for others.

I hope I have convinced you that I truly believe in the importance of the men in my life. And I firmly believe in the need of strong Christian men in this world! The enemy has done a number on families and good Christian men. But we can change that.

Having shown my true feelings about men, I have observed that many women are ready to accept a second-class citizen position in life. That second-class citizen role includes faith-related positions, allowing men to carry the more influential situations. We do that without considering how important our contribution could be to our church, our business, our families, and more.

Time can also be a factor in the decision to take on a secondary role. We are already up to our ears in busyness as wives, mothers, and other roles in society. There are only so many hours in a day, and we can overextend ourselves without realizing we have done that.

Staying in a secondary role can come into play because of what the Lord has assigned us to do and at times *not* do. If we, as women, choose to be in these secondary positions, that is one thing. It is wonderful to be obedient! I salute those women.

However, it's the women who have been made to stay in a secondary role that are not so wonderful. It's a different story when you know that God is telling you to do something and another human restricts your efforts. Like many of you, having been in that position, the frustration can become overwhelming.

It's my intention to be God's cheerleader instead of offering what may sound like a women's lib angle. I hope to encourage women to fight, fight, fight for the first-class citizen attitude God truly feels we are to Him. We will succeed, whether as a stay-at-home missionary or a missionary in China, if that is what He has asked us to do. The Bible shows how God felt about women before humans got a chance to change that thought process.

As women, we become much more comfortable accepting the enemy's interpretation of who we are than God's rendition of who we are to Him. It's more comfortable for us to think and accept the negatives: I am not important. I am fat, or I am stupid. It is harder to accept the positives: God created me. He loves me just as I am. I am His child. I am a child of a King.

Eleanor Roosevelt said: "No one can make you feel inferior without your consent.[1]

As women, we are just as much a child of God as anyone else, no better than men and no worse than men. I hope to show God's true beliefs about "I am woman" by pulling out biblical truths for all of us to

[1] As quoted in Readers' Digest, Sept 1940, 37:84

focus on. Always remember, the truth of God trumps the lies of the enemy every time. We must learn to believe those truths. A reboot or two or five will help us as women to believe these truths from our Creator.

> Psalm 68:11 supports the truth that God has a way for women to affect His kingdom.

> NIV: The Lord announces the word, and the women who proclaim it are a mighty throng.

> ESV: The Lord gives the word; the women who announce the news are a great host.

> NSA: The Lord gives the command; the women who proclaim the good tidings are a great host.

> NLT: The Lord gives the word, and a great army[2] brings good news.

When talking about women in ministry, Dr. Robin Harfouche quoted the following on a website for Patricia King's Ministries: "There is an awaking to the fact that without women we are missing 60 percent to 65 percent of the ranks of Christian workers, soldiers, evangelist, pastors, teachers, apostles, prophets that can be immediately added to ranks and numbers of the global count of Christ!"

As a lay prayer ministry counselor for several years,

---

[2] Or a host of women.

I repeatedly must work hard to get women, and some men, to learn who they are in Christ's eyes. While God does the counseling in these sessions, it is my job to turn my clients away from their everyday lives of honoring the devil more than they honor God.

We don't think about the fact that when we believe the negatives of the devil more than we believe God's truths, it is an *unintentional* way of honoring the devil more than we honor God. There are times I need to convince my ladies that God always tells the truth and Lucifer always lies.

When we honor people, be it God, Satan, or our hero, we allow them to change our lives. They change our lives through how they think and how they use those thoughts in their lives. We hold them in high esteem and want to modify our lives to equal how they live theirs.

Many of us live our lives each day believing Satan before we believe God. It's not because we are bad people. We haven't recognized who we are to believe in our way of living and our way of thinking. We simply think that we are reasoning the way we are in each instance because it's the way we normally think about things.

It doesn't occur to us that Lucifer can influence our brains. By that influence, the enemy can alter our thinking and actions and therefore how we live our lives. Not only can Satan affect our lives, but we also buy into the negative thoughts quickly and easily, without a fight. We don't stop and question our thinking or how we are acting. No one who is a Christian can be possessed by Lucifer. He can, however, influence us in a variety of ways.

We don't stop to ask, "Is this the way God would want me to handle this situation?" It is easier to slide into the negatives from Lucifer than fight for the positives from our Lord. Some have not heard of or have heard but don't use spiritual warfare. We don't understand that we can fight what is happening to us. As part of God's team, we will win! The passiveness does not need to happen. Second Corinthians 10:4–5 says,

The weapons we fight with are not weapons of the world. On the contrary, they have divine power to demolish strongholds. We demolish arguments and every pretension *that sets itself up against the knowledge of God,* and *we take captive every thought to make it obedient to Christ.* (emphasis added)

The Message may state the above a little clearer. As Paul is defending his ministry, the Message states:

The world doesn't fight fair. But we don't live or fight our battles that way—never did and never will. The tools of our trade aren't for marketing or manipulation, but they are for demolishing that entire massively corrupt culture. We use our powerful God-tools for smashing warped philosophies, tearing down barriers erected against the truth of God, fitting every loose thought and emotion and impulse into the structure of life shaped by Christ. Our tools are ready at hand for clearing the ground of every obstruction and building lives of obedience into maturity.

With understanding, practice and instruction, we can learn to force our thoughts and actions to align with God, not with the enemy.

It is hard to recognize when Satan takes over our focus and when it is time to stop those thoughts. We must learn to recognize that it is time to focus our thoughts on what is God's truth instead of what is in our heads or spirits at this point. We need to pause in our thinking to stop that lie we are obsessed with at the moment.

Putting a stop to Satan's thoughts may require us to state *out loud*, "My Creator would never say that about me. I won't allow this line of thinking one more minute. Be gone in the name of Jesus. Amen."

We don't recognize that what is happening today, right now, in our lives, in our heads, could be happening because of the enemy. Our worldly reasoning tells us we are just having a bad day, or a bad head day. Instead, we should learn to stop in the midst of the disruptive thoughts and ask God, "What is going on here? What is it You want me to realize about this situation? Is this something that aligns itself with the Bible? Does it represent something You would say to me?"

Then we need to take action.

Our first line of defense is the armor God has provided for us. He knew we would be in this battle the whole time we are on earth. As any good daddy would do, He provides us with help.

Finally, be strong in the Lord and in his mighty power. Put on the full armor of God so that you can take your stand against the Devil's schemes. (Ephesians 6:10–11)

There are a growing number of us who verbally pray on each piece of armor to anyone who will let us do that. Twice in Ephesians 6 it says, "Put on the full armor of God." So how does one put it on?

I feel that God has instructed me to pray on the armor with each of my clients. It felt strange at first to out loud pray on each piece. Then I found pastors and others who are doing the same thing. I invite God to come and place the armor on each person. Then I pray on out loud each piece as listed in Ephesians 6:13–17:

Therefore, put on the full armor of God, so that when the day of evil comes, you may be able to stand your ground, and after you have done everything, to stand. Stand firm then, with the belt of truth buckled around your waist, with the breastplate of righteousness in place, and with your feet fitted with the readiness that comes from the gospel of peace. In addition to all this, take up the shield of faith with which you can extinguish all the flaming arrows of the evil one. Take the helmet of salvation and the sword of the spirit, which is the word of God.

My clients tell me that, with their eyes closed, often they can see, in their mind's eye, at least one piece of armor God has placed on them. One of my ladies told me her sword was large, like an Excalibur sword. She was unable to lift it. A month or so later, after working with God to receive some healing from her past, she could lift her sword.

Over the years my ladies have seen the following:

> Helmet of Salvation: from crowns and Roman soldier helmets to a leather flier's cap that they used to wear years ago.

> Breastplate of Righteousness: from a large padded breastplate like the umpire behind home plate and metal breastplates to all-leather plates

> Belt of Truth: from a large belt like the pro-wrestler's win and men's belt size leather to strips of leather.

Shield of Faith: from a small, round, metal or large square wooden shield to head-to-toe-size metal or wooden shield, but all are moveable and manageable.

Sword, which is the word of God: from daggers and jeweled swords to double-edged straight or curved swords

Fitted with Footwear of Peace: from ballet slippers, moccasins, and combat boots to bedroom slippers.

I realize this information is a little out there for many of you. But I must write what I am experiencing from my years of many female clients. I wasn't going to include this in my writing since this is not talked about often, but God was insistent.

Hearing this from so many different people, I must wonder if God doesn't make each piece of armor specific for each person who takes the time to pray them on. Some of my ladies have told me that when they have entered a period of time that includes a more intense fight with the devil, that their armor has thickened.

And when I pray on these pieces of armor, different verbal explanations or descriptions come out of my mouth with no forethought on my part. I might talk about the physical description, or I might tell the person how God wants her to use that particular piece of armor. I have no logical or concrete explanation other than God. Believe me, I am not that creative to come up with some of the things that come out of my mouth.

Once the armor is in place, the next line of defense is a type of prayer. Spiritual warfare prayer is different from our everyday prayer to God. We are addressing Lucifer directly. We are commanding the enemy to be gone in the name of Jesus.

It requires only seconds to pray, "God, if I am under attack from Satan, I will not receive one more thing from him. Be gone, Satan, in the name of Jesus. Help me, Lord, to know when You want me to respond to something You want me to know about myself. I need to continue to be shaped into the person You created me to be. I pray these things in Your name. Amen."

Many need to understand that they are allowing Satan to affect their lives daily. They may be someone who considers him or herself to be living good, Christian lives. And they are right. These people are active Christians in their faith and in their church. Sometimes they are even pastors. They hear God, love God, and actively try to obey Him. Many times, they are doing good things in their lives and communities. But these activities only echo what God is asking them to do with their lives. Without a doubt, they are bearing lots of good fruit.

> You did not choose Me, but I chose you
> and appointed you that you should go
> and bear fruit. (John 15:16)

Because of what many of us allow to stay in our heads and spirits, we are unable to get to the full depth of what our Lord is trying to tell us. It makes it difficult to understand what God has for us to do or who He fully created us to be. While actively doing good work for God's kingdom, deep inside, we are thinking, *I am the worst pastor ever. I'm not doing enough to please God. I'll never get this right. I was a fool to think I could do this.*

In his booklet *God's Creative Power*, Charles Capps says:

> Christianity is called the *great confession,* but most Christians who are defeated in life are defeated because they believe and confess the wrong things. They have spoken the words of the enemy, and those words hold them in bondage. Proverbs 6:2 says, "... You are snared by the words of your mouth; You are taken by the word of your mouth."

As there is creative power in my Spoken Word, so is there evil power present in the words of the enemy to affect and oppress everyone that speaks them.

The enemy has so programmed the minds of people until instead of resisting him, they have just sort of buddied up with him, and begun to talk his language.

We have not taken control of Lucifer. This allows Lucifer to play with our heads in a negative way. What's worse is we have no problem believing the enemy. There is a comfort in what the enemy puts in our minds. His influence is so strong that regular prayer will not be enough to get him to leave us alone.

Neil T. Anderson and Timothy M. Warner's book *The Beginners Guide to Spiritual Warfare*[3] can help put this process into perspective. In the chapter "A

---

[3] Anderson, Neil, & Warner Timothy M, *The Beginner's Guide to Spiritual Warfare.* (Ventura CA: Regal from Gospel Light, 2000).

Reluctant Warrior," the authors talk about Peter's advice.

> Be alert and of sober mind. Your enemy
> the devil prowls around like a roaring
> lion looking for someone to devour. Resist
> him, standing firm in the faith, because
> you know that the family of believers
> throughout the world is undergoing the
> same kind of sufferings. (1 Peter 5:8–9)

To me this scripture is confirming that not only is the devil to be acknowledged in your spiritual life but that he can destroy you. And that it is not just you, but all your brothers and sisters in Christ who will experience the same treatment from him. Plus, we need to do something actively to resist him.

In the chapter on "What Is Spiritual Warfare?"[4] Anderson and Warner define it as:

> If spiritual warfare is not just going
> around rebuking the devil and getting rid
> of demons, what is it? The primary bat-
> tle is between the kingdom of darkness
> and the kingdom of God, between the
> Antichrist and the Christ, between the
> father of lies and the spirit of truth; and
> we are in that battle whether we like it or
> not. The primary location of that battle
> is our minds. Either we believe the lies
> that keep us in bondage or we believe the
> truth that sets us free. So, we define spir-
> itual warfare as the battle for the mind.

---

[4] Ibid., 38.

As women, we are particularly susceptible. Lucifer knew it at the beginning of time. Since the time of Eve, Lucifer figured out how he can use women for his kingdom. I remember this story about Satan as told by one of the TV pastors in his/her sermon. It went something like this.

Why do you think that Satan picked Eve to trick instead of Adam? Adam was the head of the household. He was the man of the family. Yet Eve was the one Lucifer chose to influence. I believe it was because Satan already understood the weight that a woman carries within the family.

Today, women are often the targeted ones in advertisements because they are the decision makers. Women are the major influence of how the family will function. Satan knew that if he could convince Eve, Adam would follow suit.

Another example of a woman being used by the enemy is in Jenetzen Franklin's "Power of Vision" sermon. He talks about the story of Samson (Judges 13–16). Samson was born after an angel came to his childless parents. The angel gave them instructions as to how to raise this child to be a Nazirite. Meaning, Samson was born to be in the service of God. He grew, and the Lord blessed him, (Judges 13:24). Again, this sermon went something like this.

Samson fell deeply in love with a Philistine woman and married her. While he was away, Samson's father gave Samson's Philistine wife to one of his Philistine companions (Judges 14:20, 15:1–2). This set up the hatred that Samson needed later to kill the Philistines.

When the Philistines wanted to learn the secrets about how Samson maintained his strength, they used the knowledge that Samson favored Philistine women. Enter Delilah.

As I think most, if not all, of us know, Delilah tricked Samson into revealing his secret. He was captured by the Philistines, and they plucked out his eyes. Samson prayed, God responded, and Samson won a victory for God, killing all the Philistines in the temple.

Satan uses women like Delilah and Potiphar's wife (Genesis 39) to raise havoc with men. While being a woman used to do harm is not one of the labels any of us would prefer to carry, it is a given fact that some of us deserve that label. Unfortunately, there are those of us, including me at one time, out there who seem to lean to the dark side at least at some point in our lives. And that puts a smile on the enemy's face when he can use us for his army instead of God's army.

The enemy realizes the end time is near. He is fighting harder to keep us away from our true Lord and the calling/job God has given us to do while we are on earth. If the enemy can keep us fearful, doubting, and feeling rejected, he can keep us from doing God's calling on our lives to the best of our ability. We are more willing, subconsciously, to do Satan's bidding at times simply because it is a more comfortable role for us. It is so hard to believe the good over the bad about ourselves.

It is my job for the rest of my life to snatch people, particularly women, away from Lucifer's world and hand them over to God's kingdom. There are times when I need to help them learn how to get Lucifer out of their heads and out of their spirits. We all need to be taught how to keep our true Lord foremost in our lives. This book is part of this assignment.

For years I had been filing things in my computer and in my desk drawer and putting notes on little pieces of papers for "someday." Then, suddenly, I felt God nudge me: "It's time. Let's bring it all together and add to it." There were times I would be watching a TV pastor or reading a devotional that God would tell me things. He would say, "This should be in your book." Or "You need to go back to this section of your book and enter this in that area."

When I would finish a section of this book and wonder where I should go next, within a few days, again, from the TV, a book, or wherever, an idea would drop into my head. God also surrounded me with people for support. He organized my life so it was easy to take the time to do what He was asking me to do. For years I would be seeing six to eight women at a time for counseling purposes. Lately, I have two.

No matter what happens to this book, I know that I know that whomever is supposed to benefit from this writing will. The right person may receive what God intends for them to receive just by reading this book as a favor to me. I have asked others in my life to read and comment or critique it for me before publication.

Maybe this book is for one of my dear helpers, or for one of my relatives or friends. Or maybe the intended person will not read this book until after I am dancing my way around heaven. I also know that I know that since this book is God driven, it will reach its purpose.

2

The Bible Version of "I Am Woman"

When Jesus was on earth, He did nothing to indicate to the world that women were second class citizens in His mind. For example, He picked a woman, Mary Magdalene, at one of the most critical times in His life, to be the disciple to announce His resurrection.

Yet somewhere along the way, we have been made to feel like we should not be pastors or leaders of the church because we are women. We feel we can't oversee ministries or programs that allow others to learn more about what God has for them to do.

In addition, we become comfortable with the thought that a male would do a better job because— we stop there, often unable to come up with a very valid reason because, other than, I am woman. Many women finish that statement with, "Well, I just know I could not do that, that's all" or "Let Harold (because he is a man) handle that."

When I was a senior in high school, my class teacher allowed me to be the first female business manager for the class play. But just in case, also for the first time, he appointed an assistant manager. As you can guess, that assistant manager was a boy. I was never sure what he was supposed to be doing, and neither did he. Thankfully, it all went well.

Another woman specifically assigned a role typically reserved for men is Esther. Queen Esther saved the Jewish people. There were plans in place to kill all the Jewish people. God assigned a woman to deal with it.

Esther: The Second Queen of Xerxes. An Annual Jewish Festival or Holiday Is Named in Her Honor.

Esther got her chance to save her people because of another queen who got fired. We will talk about Vashti, the queen who got fired, later (Esther 1, 2:1). Because of Vashti's act of defiance, it was decided that a search should be made for the most beautiful maidens in the area. The outstanding one among them would be a replacement for Queen Vashti (Esther 2:2–4).

We are introduced to Esther, also known as Hadassah (Esther 2:5–7). The maidens were entrusted to Hegal, who oversaw the harem. Esther found favor with Hegal. This favor helped her to be in a position for God's purpose for her, although at this point Esther had no idea what her purpose was to be (Esther 2:8–9). She had not revealed her nationality to anyone at the palace (Esther 2:10).

Over a year's time, there were various things that needed to happen before a queen was chosen. During that year, Esther began to stand out to King Xerxes. She became his favorite. Esther became queen (Esther 2:11–18).

Wisdom was one of Esther's strong suits (gifts from God), and she used that wisdom many times as queen.

Her uncle, Mordecai, found out about a conspiracy to kill King Xerxes and told Esther about it (Esther 2:19–23). Esther told the king but gave the credit of saving the king to Mordecai. This would provide a reason, in the future, for Mordecai to become honored by the king.

A later conspiracy included a plot to kill all the Jewish people. Since no one knew that Esther was a Jewish woman, including Haman, the man planning the plot, or the king, no one realized that the queen was one of the people who would be killed. Mordecai tried to persuade Esther to help prevent the annihilation of all the Jewish people, but she was reluctant to do so (Esther 4:1–17).

Just to approach Xerxes could mean Esther's death. Mordecai's talk with Esther to try to persuade her to help resulted in one of the most-quoted scriptures.

> "And who knows if perhaps you were made Queen for such a time as this?"
> (Esther 4:14 NLT)

Esther fasted and prayed for three days. She asked others to fast along with her, for Esther to find favor with King Xerxes. She did find that favor and survived this event. Not only did she survive but found a way to save her heritage and people as well (Esther 5:1–8).

Haman was instrumental in the desire to kill all the Jews and to also kill Mordecai separate from the annihilation of the Jews (Esther 5:9–14). Esther, after finding favor with King Xerxes, used her wisdom. She developed a plan to expose Haman. It took an in-depth plan, but Esther saved her people and her uncle (Esther 7:1–10).

The festival of Purim is still celebrated in certain cultures each year, because of Esther's strength in God and her success in saving the Jewish people (Esther 8:11–12, 9:24–26).

Dr. David Jeremiah has a book marker that I hold close to my heart. It states: "*I* was created for such a time as this" (emphasis added). And so were you!

God has you here on this day, in this century, in whatever area you are living in for such a time as this. So why are you here, and why are you reading this? What is it He has for you to do, at least for now, that he decided this is where and when you are to be alive?

Esther found her purpose, and so will you. Spend time with God, and He will reveal it when it is time. In the meantime, all that you are living through is preparation for that purpose. Finding the answer to the question of purpose will bring you unbelievably great joy and freedom!

Don't know what your purpose is yet? Do what you do best and enjoy doing. When you do that, it affects others around you with the love we are to give each other. Your purpose can be as simple as sending cards to anyone who could use one. Or your purpose today may be to smile at the checkout lady at the grocery store. One of my ladies who is wheelchair bound with MS has become a prayer warrior for anyone who needs prayer.

> Be devoted to one another in brotherly love. Honor one another above your-selves. (Romans 12:10)

This verse doesn't give you specific directions as to how to do this. Just keep putting one foot in front of the other until you walk yourself through your purpose and right into heaven to spend eternity with your Creator.

Paul, like Jesus, honored women. Paul sent greetings to women and to churches meeting in a woman's home (Colossians 4:15): "Give my greetings to the brothers and sisters at Laodicea, and to Nympha and the church in her house."

Note that Paul doesn't add or acknowledge that the home church should have a male as an assistant pastor just in case. (Emoji: humble smiling face.) He only acknowledges Nympha and *her* house church. Were there men in that church that made that church better in many ways. *Absolutely*!

Many of us remember Genesis 1:26 (NIV):

> Then God said, "Let us make man in our image, in our likeness, and let *them* rule over the fish of the sea and the birds of the air, over the livestock, over all the earth, and over all the creatures that move along the ground."

Moses, who is given credit for writing Genesis, didn't write, "Let's create man and woman and each will have an individual job description." *They* were equal in *their* assignment.

In Genesis 1:27, Moses went on to say, "So God created man in his own image, in the image of God he created him; male and female he created them."

On the fifth day of creation, not only did God bless them equally and give them the same assignments, but He even felt that "and it was good" (Gen 1:31).

God's seal of approval trumps HGTV's or Good

Housekeeping's (the world's) seal of approval. God said male and female are equal. The world, with the help of Lucifer, has defined the difference in male and female and changed the original rule.

Understandably, a five-foot female cannot lift the same amount as a six-foot male. And trust me, I do know the anatomical differences in our bodies and their individual functions. Get a grip here. You know very well what I am referring to in this area of equality.

At the time of this writing, women still make seventy-five cents to each dollar of a male in our paychecks. And the world still has not figured out yet that if a woman can run a household, juggle the kids' schedules with her own and her husband's while squeezing the financial needs of the family out of their paychecks, she certainly could handle being the president of the United States. Oops, did I just slip back into woman's rights again? Focus, Darci.

In John 11:1–12,19, we are told about the story of Lazarus, whom God has raised from the dead. The story about Lazarus and his two sisters, Martha and Mary, is a common story we have heard since childhood. Many who are not that familiar with the Bible can quote this story.

But how many of us can quote the story of Tabitha, also known as Dorcas? Acts 10:36–43 tells about a woman who was a disciple and who did so much good for the poor and the community. To paraphrase, Tabitha became ill and died. The disciple Peter was summoned to the house. He observed all the grieving that was going on and decided to act. Like Lazarus, Tabitha was brought back to life, and her story became known over a wide area during biblical times.

Why do few of us know that story? Maybe because

Jesus raised Lazarus from the dead instead of a disciple named Peter. Or maybe it was that Lazarus happened first, before Tabitha. Or could it be because she was a woman and not as important as Lazarus?

Yes, I meant what I said about this not being a woman's rights book for women of the Bible. I am only bringing up a point to consider. Who am I to say which story should be more known than the other? It is not mine to judge the reason for the difference in popularity of these two stories.

This may be a good place to remember Matthew 7:1–2. If you don't already know it by heart, and you need to read it:

> Do not judge, or you too will be judged.
> For in the same way you judge others,
> you will be judged and with the measure
> you use, it will be measured to you.

There is a great book titled *Why Not Women?*[5] written by Loren Cunningham and David Joel Hamilton. It was given to me by one of my early mentors who, as of this writing, is the female half of the lead pastoral couple of a large growing church. This book really helped me define who I am in God's eyes.

There is a scripture used often by many who are trying to explain why they believe a woman should *not* be a pastor or leader in a church. They feel if they quote scripture, that will prove their point that women are not supposed to be pastors or leaders in the church.

I remember working in the welcome center in the

[5] Cunningham, Loren and Hamilton, David Joel, *Why not Women?*(Seattle, WA: YWAM publishing), 2000, 185.

church I was attending at the time. A new couple came to our church that Sunday to see if they fit in because they were searching for a new church home. The wife was horrified that not only did we have people waving flags during the music, but we also commissioned a female pastor during our service.

"What's the idea behind those flags? And why are you making a woman a pastor? What kind of church is this?" asked the wife indignantly as her husband sank lower into his seat. "How could you even call yourselves a church with a woman as a pastor?"

Following is the scripture she and many others use thinking they are proving their point that women are not to be part of God's ambassadors. In my NIV study Bible, 1 Corinthians 14:33–35 states,

> For God is not a God of disorder but of peace. As in all the congregations of the saints, women should remain silent in the churches. They are not allowed to speak, but must be in submission, as the Law says. If they want to inquire about something, they should ask their own husbands at home; for it is disgraceful for a woman to speak in the church.

In *Why Not Women?*, each chapter lists the author of that chapter. David Hamilton is designated as author of the chapters addressing women speaking in church. He advises an in depth look at many aspects of these scriptures.

> As with any study of the Bible, we need to look at who is speaking?

In this case, Paul.

Who is he speaking to?

He is addressing the churches in Corinth.

What is taking place in the story?

**There is disruption and disorder occurring in the churches in Corinth which includes women, prophets and those who speak in tongues.

Mr. Hamilton points out that there were three groups Paul was addressing to "be silent."

To those who speak in tongues "be silent" (1 Corinthians 27–28)

If anyone speaks in a tongue, two- or at the most three- should speak, one at a time and someone must interpret. If there is no interpreter, the speaker should keep quiet in the church and speak to himself and to God.

To the prophets "be silent" (1 Corinthians 29–33)

Two or three prophets should speak, and the others should weight carefully what

is said. And if a revelation comes to someone who is sitting down, the first speaker
should stop. For you can all prophesy in
turn so that everyone may be instructed
and encouraged. The spirits of prophets
are subject to the control of Prophets. For
God is not a God of disorder but of peace.

To the women "be silent" (1 Corinthians
33–35) See ** page 35

Mr. Hamilton goes on to say, "It is dishonest to
single out the command directed to the women and
make it more of an absolute than the command given
to those who speak in tongues or to the prophets. Why
have we been obsessed with the third example of orderly conduct and ignored the first two?"

Mr. Hamilton continues, "Look at the first two examples. It's obvious Paul's 'be silent' wasn't an 'absolute
-forever-under-every-circumstance-and-at-all-times'
injunction against those who spoke in tongues or those
who prophesied. No, in the same passage he wrote,
'Be eager to prophesy, and do not forbid speaking in
tongues.' (v.39) The ministry gifts were not to be per-
manently silenced but were to be exercised 'in a fitting
and orderly way'. (v.40) The same is true regarding the
women. Paul was not telling women to refrain from all
public ministry. To force such an interpretation does
violence to the integrity of the text."

As an additional view on these scriptures, in my
NIV study Bible in the footnotes for the explanation of
these verses in 1 Corinthians 14:34–35 the following
is written: "See note on 11:3–16. Some believe that in
light of 11:3 there is a God-ordained order that is to

be the basis for administration and authority. Women are to be in submission to their husbands both at home (see Ephesians 5:22) and in the church (see v. 34; 1 Timothy 2:11–12) regardless of their particular culture. According to this view, a timeless order was established at creation (see note on 11:5–6)."

The footnote continues, "Others maintain that Paul's concern is that the church be strengthened (v. 26) by believers showing respect for others (see vv. 30–31) and for God (see v. 33) as they exercise their spiritual gifts. Such respect must necessarily take account of accepted social practices. If within a particular social order, it is disgraceful for a woman to speak in church—and it was in this case (v. 35)—then she shows disrespect by doing so and should remain silent. There were occasions, though—even in this culture—for women to speak in church. For example, in 11:5 Paul assumes that women pray and prophesy in public worship. Thus, his purpose, according to this view, was not to define the role of women but to establish a fitting (vv. 34–35) and orderly (vv. 27–31) way of worship (v. 40)."

Last, my study Bible version finishes the footnotes with, "Still others say that in this context Paul is discussing primarily the disruption of worship by women who become involved in noisy discussions surrounding tongues-speaking and prophecy. Instead of publicly clamoring for explanations, the wives were to discuss matters with their husbands at home (cf. v. 35). Paul does not altogether forbid women to speak in church (see 11:5). What he is forbidding is the disorderly speaking indicated in these verses."

As you can see, it takes time and digging to interpret what is happening and what is being said. It also takes time to get to know the Bible and how it reads. When you pick any genre, like mysteries, for instance, you learn the rhythm of how a mystery in general goes. There is always a good guy or guys and bad guys. The bad guys are winning at first. Then the good guys come to the rescue and win in the end. There is lots that happens in between, but in general, that's the way each mystery reads.

Well, the Bible is the same way. The more you read, the better you are at understanding it. It's great to be a part of a group that gets together to talk about the Bible. There are so many unanswered questions about the Bible. Hearing other thoughts and ideas can be helpful.

Reading the Bible may not be as much fun as reading a mystery. But with a little help, thought, and desire, you can read the Bible for a reason that is individual to you. That reason brings life to the stories in the Bible, which produces a strong desire in you to become more familiar with the Bible and its stories

Another strong desire that creates a reason to become more familiar with the Bible is to learn more about God. Since there is no longer a flesh-and-blood representation on earth, how else will you be able to become friends with God? Learning more about the Father, Christ Jesus, and the Holy Spirit takes time and reading.

Each of you will find a way to pursue the Bible in your own way and for your own reason. Just follow God's nudging's along the way. He will lead you into His own plan of action.

He nudged me to read the Bible cover to cover each year for five years in a row. One of the ladies I was mentoring was nudged by God as to which book to read when. Depending upon what was happening in her life, she might be nudged to read Hebrews from start to finish for a while. Then she would be nudged by God to switch to Job for a period of time.

Another lady had small children to raise and little time of peace to read the Bible. If she got up early before her children to read the Bible, she would fall asleep. If she waited until kids were in bed at night, her husband was a delightful distraction. While she felt bad (not guilt, which comes from Satan) and continued to look for time in the Bible, it was not until her children were older that God nudged her into a plan.

There are CDs of the Bible you can listen to in your car when you are driving. But again, if you have children, they have their own music and interest. A friend of mine with low sight issues is thrilled to be able to use CDs at home, all in God's time and all as a part of God's plan. If you keep searching and trying to find a way, your turn will come. Obeying what God nudges us to do is another issue.

It is sort of like writing this book. Usually a couple times a week, God would have me up around 3:00 a.m. and would nudge me to write. Obedience at times was easier than at other times. However, I would find that I was more creative at 3:00 a.m. than at 3:00 p.m. It was also of interest to me that when I obeyed, I did not feel tired during that day. But other days, even when rolling over and sleeping through the night, I would feel tired or at least sluggish. Hmmm

3

The Bible

Let's talk about the Bible itself for a moment. Second Timothy 3:16 says, "All Scripture is God-breathed and is useful for teaching, rebuking, correcting and training in righteousness."

Some of you who are reading this may not be as comfortable trusting the Bible as others may be. You have heard these questions asked many times. How can you trust that the Bible is really what it claims to be? How can you trust what is written when it has been written by more than one person and over a long period of time? I can't understand what the Bible is saying, so how can I possibly believe it?

I am sure some of you can list a lot more questions than I have here, so let's do some basic and general looking at the Bible. All the statistics and information to follow are easily found online. Many of you will already know the following information.

First, let me encourage you to find the right translation for you. By translation, I mean version. Understanding King James Version (KJV) was nearly impossible for me as a young Christian. By using the

NIV (New International Version) or other versions, I could better understand what was being said.

At this stage of my life, as a more mature Christian, there are times you will find me sitting at my table with not only NIV and KJV but an Amplified Version and The Message open to compare a scripture that I do not understand clearly. So, if the Bible you are using is not working for you, try another version or translation. The different translations can be added to your iPhone, tablet, or electronic devise for free for online use or downloaded for a small fee.

If you need other assistant devices, add those to your hard copy of the Bible. It may be something like large print or whatever you need to make reading the Bible easier for you. I enjoy reading it off my phone or Kindle. It makes me feel techy. I truly am technically challenged; my grandchildren are my consultants. It makes me feel more up to date to use my iPhone or Kindle in church instead of a hard copy of the Bible.

There are study Bibles with additional information at the bottom of the page for you to better understand what you just read. You can also find Bibles with divided pages. One half of the page is NIV, for instance, and the other side of the same page is The Message. Many other combinations of types of Bibles are available for you to choose from if you need something different than what you have now. Anything to appease those feelings that, right or wrong, make us react in a negative way to the Bible.

Second, you have heard this over and over. It is old news, but it is true. The more you use something, the easier it is to become comfortable with it. That works for Bibles as well as gadgets. I have spent a lot more time reading the KJV, which could have been written in Greek as far as I was concerned when I was a new Christian. Now it has become a delight to read for me even if it is not my first pick of Bible version when I do read the Bible. It has become the version I use as a final read to pull a particular scripture together for me. Yes, we all need to spend more time in the Bible, including me. But if you are still not sold on spending more time in the Bible, you are not alone.

There are things you can do to help you spend more time in the Bible. You could join a Bible study at your church that helps you to get more involved in the Bible in a more entertaining way. There are so many great Bible study teachers out there. With a little experience, you will be able to pick the one teacher who speaks loudest and easiest to you.

I love to dig deep and get way down into the nitty-gritty of the study, dissecting every word and thought. To some people, that would turn them off, and they might not finish the study. It's too much work for them. Look around at who is teaching the study. Find out how long it takes to finish the study. Research other questions like, what is the topic, and how will this study fit into my schedule the best?

Ask your Christian friends, "Who do you like as a Bible teacher? Why do you like them? Who do you avoid? Why do you avoid them?" Do your homework before you receive any homework, before you start a study, only to find it's confusing or wrong for you. You might wind up quitting out of frustration instead of finishing the study. That frustration can immediately flip you into thinking all Bible studies are impossible or a pain. How often have I heard, "I tried Bible studies, and they are not for me"? Later I find out, after asking more questions, that they tried one study and stopped with that one experience.

Another concept that is hard to put into real-life action is the statement that the Bible is the living word. I found I can read a scripture and get one thing out of it and my best friend can read the same scripture and get another meaning out of it. Then a lady I am mentoring can read the same scripture and get an entirely different and third meaning.

Along comes someone like Beth Moore, who finds things in scripture that I did not see even though I have read that same scripture a hundred times before. After Beth Moore translates it, the meaning becomes so obvious that I can't understand why I missed that same meaning all those times. This concept of different people reading the same scripture and getting different meanings from it adds to the statement made that the Bible can be confusing or contradictory.

What I have come to understand is that we each translate the scripture in our own way. How we understand it is correct for who we are and what we are living through right now. God talks to each of us. He meets us right where we are. That same scripture meant one thing to me when I was fifty. It is what I needed to hear from God at that time. Today, that same scripture relays a different message to me, which is exactly what God wants me to get out of it today.

This is a hard concept to accept, especially for those of you with scientific minds. A plus B always equals C in the scientific world. It's hard to work with a concept where A plus B might equal D, with C no longer applying to the present situation. The scientific mind is much more comfortable with A always equaling the same thing. And B always equaling the same thing. Thus, A plus B always equals C since it always equals the same thing.

I have a friend who married a real-life unsaved rocket scientist. Concrete theories and exacting measurement could mean life or death to his work situation. Trying to get him to change his way of analyzing when it comes to the Bible has been nearly impossible to do.

It will take some work for you to spend time talking with others whose minds work differently than yours. While it can be a challenge, it is well worth the effort. It can become interesting to hear how others think. I might never have thought of that angle, but by doing so, it made me realize something I needed to mull over, at least for a short time, then either file it or dismiss it. I may or may not use it, or I may learn something from it.

To be sure we are all on the same page, to some extent, with our knowledge of the Bible, here is some basic information researched from the internet.

The Bible was written over fifteen hundred years ago. There are sixty-six books in the Bible divided into the Old Testament and the New Testament. Four hundred years passed between the Old Testament and the New Testament. The Old Testament holds a lot of prophecy that is proven later in the New Testament. Following are some examples.

Old Testament

When Israel was a child, I loved him, and *out of Egypt I called my son.* (Hosea 11:1)

New Testament

Fulfilled

So, he got up, took the child and his mother during the night and left for Egypt, where he stayed until the death of Herod. And so was fulfilled what the Lord had said through the Prophet? "Out of Egypt I called my son." (Matthew 2:14–15)

Old Testament

He was assigned a grave with the wicked, and *with the rich in his death,* though he had done no violence nor was any deceit in his mouth. (Isaiah 53:9)

New Testament

Fulfilled

As evening approached, *there came a rich man* from Arimathea, named Joseph, who had himself become a disciple of Jesus. Going to Pilate, *he asked for Jesus' body,* and Pilate ordered that it be given to him. (Matthew 27:57–58)

The Old Testament is before Christ (BC). The New Testament is written about the time Christ lived and after Christ died (AC). The Bible was written by about forty people, and there are still books that are not totally proven as to who wrote them. These forty were from all walks of life, all of which adds to questions of the integrity of the Bible in some people's minds. And I was one of those!

Remember what happened when we played the game where someone whispers a sentence in the first person's ear? That sentence is passed down from person to person by whispering into the next person's ear. Remember the fun of hearing what came out of the last person's mouth in comparison to what was whispered into the first person's ear? In my mind, this was how the Bible got written. The writers of the Bible heard one thing but then possibly wrote something else. I needed to understand more about the Bible to be sold on it—a lot more!

My questions included, "How could it be the word of God? How could God have written it? How could so many different people writing it not mess it up like we did in that game? Prove it to me."

If that is you, it will take a lot more information to prove the Bible to you. You will need more understanding than what I have written here in this part of the book. More time in the study of how the Bible was written, for instance, should be explored. You will need more knowledge to help you with the concept of the Bible being the word of God.

The purpose of this book is the focus of women of the Bible yesterday and today. Taking everyone's time who is reading this book to add volumes of information here which may be required for some to accept the Bible is not logical, as Mr. Spock would say.

But I hope there is enough written here to encourage you to look further into the Bible if you need to do that to be convinced. Yet, I hope I have provided enough to allow you to proceed with reading this book and be at peace about moving on for now.

After getting whatever information we believers needed to help us understand the Bible, many of us could come to the same conclusion. We considered that forty different people, from different ages and different backgrounds, writing so many years apart, yet providing enough cohesiveness to the same story, had to mean something. We acknowledged more than one biblical writer would write about the same story, with the same characters. Some might have a little more or a little less about the same story. Or you could tell that they were looking at the same story but from a different perspective. However, they could provide enough like information about that story, or its characters, that you knew the story had to be the same situation.

We could tell the story had a deep concept for us to take away from that story. There was something important that we were to learn from that story. The writers all came together in a cohesive way, which had to mean the Bible was not your typical book. The Bible had to be a product of a supernatural situation. That supernatural situation can only be God.

One long weekend I flew to meet my brother at his home. His wife was away for the weekend, so we had lots of time to talk about the good old days—or in our case, the not-so-good old days. As we talked and focused on the same situations, we would find because we each had a different perspective, the story would look slightly different to each of us.

It didn't mean the story wasn't true. The story was true. We knew we could relate enough about the story to know the basics of the story were the same. It had been observed by my brother and by me since we both lived it at the same time, in the same place. Yet that same story had a bit of a twist depending which one of us was retelling the story. This is an example of how the Bible was written by different people yet could still be accurate.

If you know anyone who has written a song or written a book, you will hear them say something like, "It just came to me. I don't know where the words or music came from. It just happened." Those people who speak in public may tell you, "I couldn't believe what came out of my mouth. There was no thinking involved in what came out of my mouth. It just came out."

There are times we sit to write or stand to speak, and there is a feeling inside us that can't be explained. We know what we know, or think we know, about that subject. Suddenly, out of our mouth, or appearing on the paper before us, is information we did not come up with on our own. After we hear it or read it we know it to be true and real. Sometimes even looking back on those words or music we say to ourselves, "Wow, I sounded really good. I wonder where that came from?"

Those people are more likely to be able to understand how the Bible was written and how it truly is the word of God. It is a much harder concept for those who have not experienced something like has been mentioned here. Each one of those forty writers had experiences like this. God would direct their writing and allow His words to come out of each of them when they wrote.

Those of you who do prayer ministry in your churches have similar stories. Each Sunday you can come away not knowing why you said what you said to some of the people who came forward for help. Yet they commented back to you that you said something they really needed to hear. They tell you that you hit the nail on the head with your advice.

Many of us who pray for others have experienced the same thing. Then they come back to us at a later date to let us know how important our prayer was for the situation. We just smile and nod because we can't remember a word we said to them. It was because they were words we received from God, not from our own minds. These experiences help to explain how the Bible was written.

I hope that as you find others who can tell you their experiences face-to-face that trusting the Bible will become easier and more enjoyable.

Moving On!

Eventually, as I spent more time with God, more time in the Bible, and more time with more mature Christians willing to teach, my cynicism changed. My weaknesses became my strengths.

> Whose weakness was turned to strength.
> (Hebrews 11:34)

I do sincerely hope that I have given those fellow cynics who are not sure that the Bible is the word of God, at least a level of comfort with the Bible to be able to continue reading this book, so let's do move on.

4

Mary, Did You Know?

In some ways, I went back to school in my late fifties. While taking classes to learn to do the type of counseling that I do, I started experiencing flashback scenes. I thought PTSD (post-traumatic stress disorder) was only for soldiers. Now, having conquered many things, I still feel my experience with PTSD was minor compared to what soldiers must deal with. The horrors of war must be extremely life altering. I know that some of my ER experiences were life altering for me, and they were mild in comparison.

However, at the time I was experiencing my own PTSD, it was greatly affecting my life. What I had lived through as a child had taken my mind into a place that I could not handle. I totally displaced those experiences in my mind up till now. Up until the age of fifty-four, I had no idea that I had experienced sexual abuse. God brought it back to me later in life for me to heal from my past. He knew I had to relive those experiences to heal.

As these flashbacks became more real and occurred more often, there were several topics I needed to better understand. I knew that I needed more knowledge about satanic cults, amnesia, counseling, faith, satanic ritual abuse, and parts, personalities, or alters. It may help all of us to have the same level of knowledge of these areas. It is here that I have chosen to give a basic explanation of these areas as I understood them at that time.

This part of the book is information as I interpreted it at that time and may not at all resemble what you know about each area. We all interpret life and things we learn in individual ways. Much of our learning depends upon our past experiences, our level of intellect, and the resources available for our research. There are many of you with a wealth of knowledge on all these topics who would do a better job of explaining them. For you to better identify with me at the time of my therapy years, it would help for you to understand my level of knowledge at that time.

I was telling a female pastor friend of mine who mentored me during this time how I felt. I was in what I called my "convent phase." Back when movies were still in black and white, I had watched a movie where nuns were the focus. They were strictly kept within the confines of their church and convent, with little to no outside activities.

At this point, I had stopped counseling others. I had no social life to speak of and spent my time studying. I studied what I was taught in various classes I was taking. Plus, I was being given articles and information through various mentors. I was involved in Bible studies as well. The internet was available but certainly not the resource it is today.

Looking back, though, I think I learned more at this time in my life than all my structured education put together. I wanted to learn. I needed to learn. I couldn't get enough information.

Remember, this is how I was interpreting these topics at this particular time in my life. I am sure you may have other ideas on these topics. Even for me, looking at these topics now, I have a different take on some of them.

Satanic Cults

There are many types of satanic cults and many names that represent satanic cults. At times, the people involved in them do not realize who they are worshiping. Other times, they know exactly who they are worshiping. Various churches acknowledge cults are present and active, and others do not.

The cult my family was involved in was one of those that the men, in general, did not know who they were worshiping until they reached a certain level within that cult. My grandfather was one of the head "poo-pahs," so my family from my father's level upward knew exactly who they were worshiping. Certain satanic rituals were in place and had been for generations. I like to think those rituals are no longer practiced.

With my father's and grandfather's approval, I was used as one of the virginal sacrifices in some of their generational rituals. While I participated in them from about the age of three or four until twelve years of age, I had no memory of them until about my mid-fifties. How selective amnesia works will be explained later in this book.

What I lived through had been so traumatic to me that I had suppressed it until I took classes to do the counseling that I do with women. Meaning until I hit my mid-fifties, I thought I lived one sort of life, only to find out everything was a lie.

There was proof that my grandmother and mother were aware, which will become more evident later in the book. I feel that my grandmother not only knew, she also approved and was honored that I was chosen for this.

My mother, on the other hand, while allowing it to happen, I think, felt helpless to do anything about it. By the end of my three and a half years of therapy, I finally understood that my mother's alcoholism and clinical depression probably stemmed from her inability to help me.

I have met and spent time with other women who have experienced what I did, most through various cults. Thankfully, God brought these others into my life who helped me to learn I was not making these things up. I was not crazy. As I learned of their experiences, I saw where my memory of what happened to me coincided with their lives as children.

I needed to learn more about satanic cults as I unraveled my past life and how it was affecting my present decisions. One of the books I used was the book *Unmasking Freemasonry, Removing the Hoodwink* by Selwyn Stevens. But in general, I soaked up what I could from the internet. There were details I had forgotten over the years about my experiences with the cult society my family attended. From my PTSD flashbacks (post-traumatic stress disorder), I would recall my family's involvement. You will learn more about PTSD also later in this book.

As I had come to understand cults (remember this is my understanding at the time of my being in therapy), these were men who had formed a secret society.

Most of the men collectively felt they were truly worshiping God in the specific cult I experienced. In reality, they were worshiping a cleverly disguised evil
one, Satan.

Only the men who were high up in this society
would understand who they were really honoring. As
in my family, the wives and children were also involved in off-shoot societies that honor Satan. These
additional followers think they are worshiping the true
God also.

I have been with some of these deceived individuals
at their death bed. They are proud that they honored
God through their time in one of these societies. They
and many of their family members never learn who
was really being honoring.

I had totally forgotten I was in a portion of the cult
for younger girls. At the time, I thought I was honoring
"the God." These are girls from the ages of twelve to
twenty-one, whose dads are cult members. It wasn't
until I started having flashbacks of my past and began to do research that I recalled being part of this
group. (See amnesia.) Before that, I had no knowledge,
at least consciously, that I was honoring the devil. My
mother was a member of a portion of the group for the
wives. My brother was part of the boys' portion, which
represent young men from ages twelve to twenty-one.

My family had belonged to this cult group for generations on my father's side. They had worked their
way up the line to a position of honor. My grandfather
and one of my uncles, in different periods of time,
were the head poo-pah of that group. Eventually, that
would allow them to know exactly who they were honoring. Even if they wanted out, and I do not know that
they did, it would have been difficult.

Another thought is that when this cult was established, what did they practice as a group? They may not have had the same practices as the present-day group had when my family was initially involved. Could the rules have changed? As I mentioned, I have hopes what I experienced is no longer happening to other young girls. You will learn more about some of these practices further on in this book.

At one point during my healing process, God provided a way for me to learn more about this group. After my uncle died, I was helping my aunt clean out the basement where my uncle had what would now be called his man-cave. We found beautiful silver items that appeared well kept and important to my uncle. My aunt and I had no idea what they were at the time.

A few weeks later I stumbled upon a TV show on *National Geographic*. It was showing, for the first time, a secret ceremony for the induction of the head poo-pah. There, were the items we found in my uncle's man cave. They were being used as part of the induction ceremony.

This is the extent of what I knew about the particular cult that my family was involved in at the time of my experience with some of their rituals. Later, after finding more and more women who had experienced the same thing I did, I have learned more about this group and other cults in existence.

Satanic Ritual Abuse (SRA)

Satanic ritual abuse is defined in the Webster's dictionary as "the *alleged* sexual abuse or murder of people, especially children, *supposedly* committed as part of satanic rituals."

Many people do not believe this type of thing has

happened or is happening in real life. As you can see
by the terms *alleged* and *supposedly* in the definition
from the dictionary, the author of this definition is one
who doubts this is real. "They" feel that those of us
who have experienced it are making it up. Or that we
dreamed it (SRA) and have thought it to be real, when
it is not. Even today there are only a minority of those
of us who lived through satanic ritual abuse who feel
safe enough or comfortable enough to talk about this
out loud to others.

We wait cautiously when a conversation seems to
be heading in that direction to see if someone else will
bring up the topic first. Only then do some of us speak
out about our experiences. There are those of us who
say little during the entire conversation other than to
discretely, with a slight nod of our head, acknowledge
that we know what is being talked about.

We all carry shame, guilt, or some unwarranted
damaging emotion that still lives inside us. Many of
us have conquered that unwarranted damaging emotion after many sessions with a counselor. Yet on days
when we feel weaker for any reason, that unwarranted
damaging emotion can raise its accusing head. At
times, we have a hard time shoving it back where it
belongs, back at Satan.

Some of us wrongly believe we deserved to be
treated like that or at least it was our fault that we
experienced the pain and abuse. We know that most
people are not going to believe us. Others, who have
not experienced SRA, have told us that we are making
this up to get attention. An even worse response, they
laugh, thinking it's too ridiculous to be true, so we
must be joking.

Those unbelievers are certainly not observing our

facial expressions or body language as we talk about it. Our nonverbal response should show them we are not joking. We understand others are very uncomfortable with the conversation. Therefore, they use the technique of laughter to move away from the subject. The subject is too taboo, too unreal, too painful to even imagine.

Those of us who have experienced some form of SRA have worked incredibly hard to get it to a place where we can deal with it out loud. While it remains in the far reaches of our brains forever, we have found a way to live with it. For some, it emotionally pains us too much to acknowledge within ourselves, let alone discuss it with others. Living with it becomes a daily challenge.

Throughout the years, I have met other women who have experienced various forms of SRA. I knew none of these women before our discussions. One of the things we do, without really thinking about it, is compare notes. I have learned that our experiences are generally quite similar. These are women from different locations, at different stages in their lives, whom I have met with on separate occasions. While we are different ages, we are all usually within a ten-year age span of each other. We can give each other similar examples of our SRA experiences.

(Side note: One of my more recent acquaintances whom I had asked to read my book and give her opinion, surprisingly, was an even better support than I anticipated. It turns out she had been one of the ladies who had walked alongside another in her congregation who had experienced SRA. While she herself could not appreciate what we lived through, she certainly knew and observed what SRA had done to the lady she was working with. I love how God picks time, places, and situations to add confirmation and support in times that we need him!)

One example of our similar experiences is that at the time of the SRA, we were all children. Another similar example is how our families have been involved in a certain type of satanic cult for generations. Some families knew they were honoring Satan. It was common knowledge in their family that they were a part of a satanic cult. Most families, in general, never find out that they are not honoring the God they think they are honoring

There are many different types of cults, each with a slightly different focus, each with a slightly different method in the rituals they perform. This accounts for the slightly different ways we might experience the abuse. Some traditions or rituals seem close to the same experience within many cults.

As an example, dripping hot wax, as part of a ritual, on various more tender parts of our bodies. When this topic came up, some of us can even distinguish which color wax was more painful than the others. White wax was slightly more comfortable, if you can call it comfortable at all. Red or black wax hurt the most. We would know, if we were not blindfolded at the time, when the abuser walked into the room carrying a black candle that we were in for extreme pain. More often, we were blindfolded and restrained in some fashion. We had no idea what was going to happen next to us, let alone the color of the wax.

I don't fault those who don't believe me or think I am making this up. It truly is beyond belief. If I hadn't lived it myself, I am not sure I would believe others either. The flashbacks I experienced, along with the visions that God provided for my healing sessions, are in line with the others who have experienced the same thing.

I can't image how we all could make up the same basic story. The only way we are saying the same thing is to have lived through it ourselves. It would seem impossible that we each could make up the same story of lies just to get attention. Very few, if any, people have published exactly what they experienced at the hands of a satanic cult. Therefore, it is unlikely that each of us has read about it and used that information to tell others what happened to us.

For me, it took a long time to stop asking Dee, my therapist, if she was sure I wasn't making this all up. At that time, I had not met anyone else who had lived through this type of abuse. It is so bizarre and unreal that even though I lived through it, I doubted myself. Over the years, since I have finished my own counseling, I have talked to even more ladies who have lived through SRA. I see relief in their eyes when they hear my story because they too thought they were making this up.

My hope is that the sexual abuse I experienced through a satanic cult is no longer occurring. However, I know there are satanic cults all over the world that are still practicing these rituals and more. White slavery, child slavery, and other types of abductions happen not only overseas but right where we live.

I could not imagine someone making this up. I did have an experience while my pastor/psychologist/mentor/friend was training me to do the type counseling I do. It was an interesting experience with one of his clients. He had been seeing her for some time. A concerned couple had graciously taken her into their home to live with them because she was unable to deal with life. As his client talked to him about her experiences, I knew she was making it up. I assumed she was lying for attention since it was not because she really experienced it.

I had not started my own counseling ministry yet. At that point, my mentor did not know that I had experienced SRA. I was sure she was lying. But my mentor had bought into her story. She, too, did not know I had experienced SRA myself. I asked my mentor if I could take the lead in the next session the following week. I did not tell him why. He agreed. I wanted him to hear her lies and not just tell him what I thought.

We started our session by just chatting in general about her abuse. I asked her if she would mind talking about some of her abuser's rituals since I was not as familiar with her story as my mentor was. She agreed. I let her talk and listened closely. When she started talking about experiencing the abuse associated with hot wax, I turned the session around in a way that shocked her and my mentor.

She complained about what she had to live through from her father, who headed up a satanic cult (not my cult but another), using hot wax on her. Yet as part of the conversation, she never really gave specifics about the abusive session or how it felt for her when the hot wax was dripped on her. So now it was my turn to asked for clarification.

"Yes," I started confidently. "I remember how hot wax felt too. Which color wax hurt you the most?"

There was stunned silence in the room. My mentor's eyes were as big as hers, both staring back at me with mouths open. I continued. "I can't decide if red or black was the worst. Could you tell which was worst for you?"

Still no one else responded. The room remained silent except for my voice. I was waiting for my mentor to stop the process, but he didn't. I wasn't sure if I had overstepped my bounds. This was my first session leading.

Continuing, since my mentor hadn't stopped me, I said, "I was always glad when the man walked in the room with the white candle in his hand, when I was lucky enough to not be blindfolded. There were times, as I am sure you experienced, that I was blindfolded and tied down. I had no idea what was going to happen to me next. The waiting, not being able to see, the vulnerable feeling of being tied down, nude and unable to flee, was almost harder to deal with than the actual pain from the hot wax. I squirmed within the bounds of the restraints, thinking if I pulled hard enough the ropes would break, hoping that by moving, the wax would miss my body or whatever was coming next would be easier."

She stammered on about candles for a few sentences. Our session continued but in a more subdued manner. She changed the subject rather quickly. Her next topic was about mental health issues that she truly did have going on.

After the session, my mentor sat there looking at me like he had never seen me before. He didn't speak for a while. He just sat there. I thought he might be upset about the session but he was not, just shocked.

When he was finally able to speak, he said, "It amazes me how God brings people together at times. What did you have as the goal of this session since you asked to lead? You must have had some specific goal in your mind."

I told him I had experienced SRA and I felt that she had not. For whatever reason she might have to do this, I felt she was lying. I wanted to test her in front of him to see how it would go. I asked him what he thought. He decided he needed to take a whole new look at the situation with this client.

Unfortunately, she never returned. She made her next appointment with him before she left. She just did not show up for her next appointment. Neither did she call to cancel. We waited for her for over a half hour.

She did not answer his phone calls throughout the following weeks as he tried to follow up with her. I was truly sorry she never showed up again because she still needed help. My hope was that she found help from someone else. Even if she never experienced SRA, she needed help with other aspects of her life as well as why she was lying about her SRA.

Amnesia

According to the Webster's dictionary, amnesia is defined as "a disturbance in the memory of stored information of variable durations, minutes to months to years, manifest by inability to recall past experiences."

WebMD defines dissociative amnesia as "occurs when a person blocks out certain information, usually associated with a stressful or traumatic event, leaving her unable to remember important personal information. With this disorder, the degree of memory loss goes beyond normal forgetfulness and includes gaps of memory for long periods of time or of memories involving the traumatic event."

Dissociative amnesia is not the same as simple

amnesia, which involves a loss of information from memory, usually as a result of disease or injury to the brain. With dissociative amnesia, the memories still exist but are deeply buried within the person's mind and cannot be recalled. However, the memories might resurface on their own or after being triggered by something in the person's surroundings.

As a nurse, not only did I understand this, but I also had patients who experienced it in varying degrees. I've watched them struggle to gain a foothold back into their life. Once they realized they had to deal with life differently than they ever imagined, they struggled to find normalcy. Everything changed. For some, as in my case, our whole past was not what we thought it was. Our whole identity changed, along with the identities of those we loved.

I did not have a clue over the years that this was in fact how I had been living. Amnesia happens to others, not to me. Several months after my father died, I started with flashbacks of my childhood while taking the classes I needed to do counseling. Not remembering any of the flashbacks as being my life, I thought I was making them up for some reason. These flashbacks were not my life.

Who totally forgets their life as a child? I knew my life as one way, only to wake up another day to discover I had it all wrong. All my life I lived feeling my past had gone one way. The people I loved were not who I thought they were. Then in my mid-fifties, I discovered my past was not at all what I thought it to be.

Even though I had helped patients deal with this, it could never be happening to me. I must be going crazy. I couldn't put this together in my mind for many weeks. I kept putting off dealing with it, until I finally felt I needed to know the truth.

Originally, I went to Dee for help to find out why I would make up these lies I was seeing in my flashbacks. These flashbacks were not the life I lived. It took three months of weekly therapy to move past the denial stage. After hard work, I finally admitted the memories were mine. The flashbacks would appear throughout the years with Dee. While I had admitted to myself that they were real, I would often ask her, "Are you sure I am not making these things up?"

Her answer was, "I have been doing this for eleven years. I have gotten pretty good at figuring out who is lying and who is not. You are not lying or making this up."

The minute I allowed myself to move on from denial and to admit this was my life, things changed. During my therapy time, I started to recall various things from my past I had forgotten. Situations I had totally forgotten through the years suddenly became very clear to me—things I had truly experienced but had, before my therapy, totally left my memory.

For example, here is one memory that came back to me as if it happened yesterday. During my time as a student nurse, my mother had driven me back to my nurse's residence after a weekend off. As we sat in the car talking, she said to me, "Now that you are a nurse and you have seen other man's penis, is your father's penis a normal size?"

I was so stunned I couldn't respond. We don't talk like this in my family. All I could think of was, *When did I see my father's penis? What do you mean I've seen my father's penis?*

I was overwhelmed trying to recall seeing my dad.

In a state of confusion and stress, I quickly blurted out, "He's normal." I had no idea why I said that.

Before those words were completely out of my mouth, I leaped out of the car, slammed the door shut, and ran into the nurse's residence. I then totally forgot that conversation for years until my days in therapy.

This conversation happened when I was nineteen or twenty years old. I never remembered it until my mid-fifties when I acknowledged the flashbacks were real. Remembering this and other flashback situations allowed me to go into deep, deep therapy. My healing process had begun!

As time went on, this memory also helped to confirm what happened to me as being real. My mother must have known about my sexual abuse, or how would she know I saw my father's penis? It additionally told me that my mother was aware of what was happening to me and did nothing to rescue me from it.

It took lots of time to heal from just this one memory. Did no one love me enough to rescue me? Mommies and daddies are supposed to love and take care of their children. What was wrong with me that they didn't want to stop this from happening? I must have deserved it.

Later in therapy, the thoughts moved on to a different level. How will I ever forgive my mom? Now I know why she drank a lot. At one point, she had become bed bound and no longer took care of my brother and me.

As a second grader, I was getting my brother and me off to school each day. I now understand that she was clinically depressed. That depression may have existed because she felt she could do nothing to rescue me.

In those days women were less likely to become

single parents. My mom had no education past high school. Not only would she have no ability to support my brother and me, but she also would have been ostracized. Single mothers were considered bad women during this era. So, she drank to keep out the thoughts of what was happening to her daughter.

As the flashbacks continued, I learned more about dissociative amnesia, which results from an emotional shock that is more than someone can handle. That shock makes you dissociate yourself from your own body when you need to do so. The trauma that I was experiencing as a child between the ages of three to twelve years old was more than I could handle. In my brain I needed to go somewhere else while the trauma was happening to me.

During my time in therapy, I was doing volunteer work in an office with a group of psychologists. I had been reading a book from the psychologists' library about dissociative amnesia. It stated that many of us who have experienced extremes in abuse resulting in dissociative amnesia heal better having experienced this form of amnesia.

Parts, Personalities, or Alters

Many of you have watched movies like *The Three Faces of Eve* or a TV show about a crazy woman with many different personalities. However, Hollywood has not done this subject justice. It is a subject that is very easy to sensationalize. It makes a great topic of interest to draw people to watch it or hear about it. It increases the ratings.

They present the multiple personalities topic in a way that provokes public interest and excitement at the expense of accuracy. This leaves those of us who are willing to share this with others openly ashamed and hesitant. Different forms of counseling use different terms for the same thing. Psychologists use the term *personalities* or *alters* for alter egos. Counselors who use prayer ministry/God as the counselor/inner healing use the term *parts*.

I feel it is biblical and has been made out to be something it is not. Having multiple personalities is something we all have. Not only do we all have parts, but God also gave them to us when He formed us. We are made in His image.

Multiple personalities can become an unhealthy mental illness that requires hospitalization when the person can no longer function in society or when the person feels these parts or personalities are making them do something they don't want to do.

But multiple personalities or parts can also be a healthy entity of our lives used for good. Most of us know that we are never made to do something we don't want to do. We cannot go kill someone or become an alcoholic because one of our parts is making us do that.

Multiple personalities are defined in the Webster's dictionary as "a *rare* dissociative *disorder* in which two or more personalities with distinct memories and behavior patterns *apparently* exist in one individual."

This is the current psychological definition still using words like *rare, disorder,* and *apparently* to show their labeling and disbelief of this topic too.

Before we talk more about multiple personalities, let me say this. There are many qualified, caring, competent psychologists who are very capable of helping you and yours when you need them, some of which are good friends of mine. In no way am I putting down anyone who uses psychology as a form of help for any type of mental health issue. I am only pointing out here the differences in our theories.

There are clients who have not been helped through using psychology that God's type of counseling, inner healing, has helped. And there have been clients I have not been able to help using inner healing or God's type of counseling who I have referred to a psychologist. And they have done well using psychology.

I have also had clients I share with a psychologist, including working along with a PhD, a doctor in psychology. We were seeing the same client at the same time but using two different techniques. Many of us go to more than one doctor.

Some people are helped by Aspirin, and some people are helped by Tylenol. Both are good products and help many people. What works for one may not work as well for the other. Both types of medication are still good products. So it is with psychology and inner healing.

Since the inner healing, theophostic, or God type of counseling is what I use and what worked extremely well on me, it is what I am addressing now. It is not as well known or understood as psychology. Quite honestly, this form of counseling, inner healing, can also be controversial depending upon whom you asked. Inner healing, or God as the counselor and me as-the-liaison, is the one I am talking about the most.

As student nurses, we were given psychology courses, and I spent three months working at a state mental hospital. I used psychology with my patients while working as an RN, so sometimes God will have me use psychology on one of my present clients. Other times He will have me use something from one of my more current courses in inner healing, which is what I am talking about here.

However, in the Bible "parts" are looked upon in a completely different light. Psalms 139:13 says: "You made all the delicate, inner parts of my body and knit me together in my mother's womb." This doesn't say in the bible that they are referring to only your organs. IE: kidney, heart. Our spiritual inner being is just as vital to our health as our physical being.

Let's look at Genesis 1:26. I am sure you have read it many times and you may even be able to recite it by heart. But look closer.

> Then God said, "Let *us* make mankind in *our* image, in *our* likeness, so that they may rule over the fish in the sea and the birds in the sky, and the livestock and all the wild animals, and over all the creatures that move along the ground." (emphasis added)

Let me ask you this: Do you believe in the Trinity? Do you believe there is a Father, Son, and Holy Spirit? Do you believe God is the Father, Christ Jesus is the Son, and that after Christ's death, He left behind the Holy Spirit or Holy Ghost to dwell within us always? Most of us do believe that. But we may not have defined that belief as completely as this until we think it through more in depth.

If there are three parts to God and we were created in His image, why would we not have parts also? We humans are often referred to as individual trinities ourselves. How often do you hear that we have three parts to us, body, mind, and spirit or soul? Do you

think it is only a coincidence that there is the concept
of a trinity for God as well as a concept of a trinity for
us as humans spoken about in literature? There are
three parts to our Creator and three parts to those
He created. Us!

Here is another biblical example of the three en-
tities that make up our heavenly Father. In Hebrews
11:32–39 we are learning about the various people
who were noted for their faith and their commitment
to the promise given to them by God. Yet these, and
others, never got to see the completion of their promise. As an added explanation, as to why they did not
receive their promise, Hebrews 11:40 says:

> Since God had planned something better
> for us so that only together with us would
> *they* be made perfect.

According to my NIV study Bible, this verse meant:
"The fulfillment for THEM, as for us, is in Christ who
is 'the resurrection and the life … All persons of faith
who had gone before focused their faith on God and
his promises. The fulfillment of God's promises to
them has now come in Jesus Christ."

Let's look at this verse in an additional way.

Since God had planned something better for us
(those who receive the promises) so that together with
us (again those of us who receive the promises) would
they (Father, Son and Holy Spirit) be made perfect.
(explanations added by me)

So, again, as in Genesis 1:26, God is referred to
as more than one entity. Again, there are three parts
of God and we are made in His image. Therefore, we
must have parts also. The KJV says:

God having provided some better thing for us (those receiving the promise), that they (Father, Son and Holy Spirit) without us (those receiving the promise) should not be made perfect. (explanations added by me)

The NLT says:

For God had something better in mind for us (those receiving the promise), so that they (Father, Son and Holy Spirit) could not reach perfection without us (those receiving the promise). (explanations added by me)

Why do Genesis 1:26 and Hebrews 11:40 use the word *they* instead of *Him*? Because God, who is the trinity, is the one being made perfect, not just Jesus or just the Holy Spirit. If it were Jesus, the word *Him* would work. Jesus is one part of God. When referring to God, God includes the Father, Son, and Holy Spirit.

If you were active in church as a child, you may have struggled with the concept of the Trinity. Some of us as adults still struggle with the concept of three parts to God. But the end results are that we need to come to the realization of when the term *God* is used, it means all three parts of God.

If you can now consider at least that we already have some parts, like God does, it's not a far stretch to believe we can develop parts as we need them. Or even more possible, that God gives us those extra parts when we need them.

Under extreme stress, like satanic ritual abuse, or fighting a war and having to kill others and watch others die, God allows us to develop or He gives us the extra parts we need to help keep our sanity or to use later in a healing purpose. Many have heard about post-traumatic stress disorder as discussed in the amnesia section earlier. Using parts can help heal some of the issues in PTSD. Yet other issues with PTSD remain for our lifetimes.

Stop here—and think about this! I can guess this might be the first time most of you have heard this theory. But God has given us logic. He has given us the ability to think and learn—the ability to think about something new to our own already established understanding. As far as I know, I am the only one with this theory of three parts to God and therefore three parts for us who have put this in writing. At least I have not read about it elsewhere. There may be rumors or conversations about this, but write-ups about this, at least for me, do not exist. But someone must begin the thought process sometime!

(Please do send me information if you know of other articles or books that support or deny this theory in writing of three parts of God so why not parts for us also. The back of this book tells you how to contact me.)

Again—I believe there are three parts to God—God the Father/Lord, Jesus the Son/Christ, and the Holy Spirit/Ghost. We were created in God's image. If He has parts, how could He *not* give us parts too?

While learning about something as shocking as satanic ritual abuse has probably blown your mind, try to move on now to this additional mind-blowing topic. Allow yourself time to put it into your brain. Don't just speed read past this part. If you take nothing else away from this book but this theory about parts as at least something to think about further, I will know that my labor over this book has not been wasted.

One last time—again—my Lord uses God, Jesus, and the Holy Spirit to function within his supernatural world. Since I was created by Him, why can I not have protector, madwoman, and Sam to help me function in my world?

These added parts come out only when they are needed. *I am never controlled by them.* I am in control each time they surface. They speak up to help me heal and then go with peace, back inside of me, no longer needing to appear once my healing is whole or complete. The parts all come together in peace inside me when my healing has been completed. This is called integration.

Many ladies I have worked with who have had parts, like me, have a variety of ways of naming them. Actually, God names them for us. Some parts will use emotions as their names, like fear or anger. Other parts use names as we would normally name our children, like Susie or Betsy.

With God's assistance, these parts will become prevalent when necessary. They help people realize something that happened to them in their past that needs to be reevaluated. Or the situation may be brought back to their memory to find out the truth about what happened. Finding the truth helps us to rid ourselves of Satan's lies.

Once these parts find peace, they retreat inside, and all come together as one. As mentioned before, this is called integration.

Here is an example of how parts can help you learn the truth about your past and promote healing in the present. One of the ladies, as a client of mine, was shocked to discover that her mother didn't hate her. All her life my client had thought her mother had hated her. She thought the reason her mother kept sending her off to her grandparents' house as she was growing up was done because her mother couldn't stand to have her around. Her mother hated her so much she got rid of her and handed her off to her grandparents.

By working with God and a part of my client that was formed inside her as a child, we learned the truth. The reason her mother kept sending her away to her grandparents was to keep her protected from her father. He had been sexually abusing her. My client was not sent away frequently to her grandparents because her mother hated her. It was because her mother loved her and was trying as best she could at that time to protect her.

The little girl part was formed because my client was unable to deal with the rejection from her mother. She felt rejected because her mom kept sending her away. Also, the part was formed because of the father's sexual abuse. The lie from the enemy my client believed all her life was that her mom sent her away because she hated her so much she didn't want her around. God's truth, in the form of the little girl part, set her straight.

Additionally, my client was so traumatized by the sexual abuse from her father that she needed other parts to deal with it all. Those parts were all dealt with separately over several sessions.

God showed my client that her mother truly loved her and was sending her away for protection purposes. The little girl part could bring back memories that my client had forgotten. She had only remembered the lies the enemy had placed in her mind about her mother. God brought the truth to surface by having the little girl part that was formed by that abuse come out and talk about the truth.

The truth was her father was sexually abusing her, and any chance the mother would get, she would send my client to her grandparents as protection. That was the best that mother could do to protect her daughter at that time. My client and her mother were then able to reestablish a meaningful mother-daughter relationship after she learned the truth.

They enjoyed a healed relationship after that session. The mother never explained to her daughter what was going on because families didn't talk about that stuff out loud. They just dealt with it quietly. No one was to know about it.

My first part really surprised me. It was a three-year-old me. I heard myself talking like a three-year-old would sound, including the sniffling.

"I hate my Pappy," Sniffle. Sniffle.

I heard those childlike words coming out of my mouth. I knew that I was speaking, but it sounded exactly like a little girl was saying it, not the adult me in the chair in my therapist office. Where did this come from? I was shocked and hesitated.

Dee changed her way of speaking to talk to the three-year-old me as any women would speak to a three-year-old. "You hate your Pappy, sweetie. Why do you hate your Pappy?"

"My Pappy hurts me." I increased the sniffling like a little girl.

"What do you mean he hurts you, honey?" Dee continued to encourage the child in me.

"He hurts me between my legs." And so, the scene

with my Pappy whipping me between my legs with a restructured coat hanger began.

Without the help of that part, I might never have learned about the truth behind my pain and severe depression. My past was why I was making the bad decisions in my life. I thought I was no better than dirt, so why should anyone think any better of me than a piece of dirt? As a matter of fact, one of the last parts I had to deal with had the name Dirt.

Eventually, as time has gone on, I have now been healed from the horrible depression, which I had experienced for years as a grown-up. Do I still have down days? Absolutely. But nothing close to the debilitating depression that kept me lying on my couch all day, unable to function. There were days I contemplated suicide. Thankfully, I never tried to kill myself.

Thank You, Lord! And thank you, Dee. This is all a part of what has drawn me to counsel others as Dee counseled me. Why would I not want to give back in my own way?

Class dismissed! Teaching time is over. There is so much more I could write about this, but "parts" is not the focus of this book. We are now all on the same level of knowledge of these topics as I was at the time of my therapy. We may not all agree with these topics, but we are at least on the same playing field. Hopefully this will help us all go through the rest of this book in an easier fashion.

I had no idea how hard the work would be for me to heal from my past. It was and is a lifelong struggle. God needed me to heal to a certain level before He could trust me with some of His most wounded children.

Counseling

There are various types of counseling. Two types are psychological and a prayer type of counseling. This second type of counseling has a diversity of names. Inner healing, theophostic, and sozo are some of those names. With this type of counseling, the approach is more God driven with some psychology mixed in to it. The traditional Christian psychologist uses psychology with a bit of God mixed in to it. Both ways have their merit and advantages.

As a nurse who has had some psychology courses, I tend to use whatever God recalls at the time. I never charge, and I never advertise. I rely entirely on God to send me whomever He chooses, using whatever means He chooses to promote healing.

For me, though, I am convinced that the inner healing type therapy brought major healing into my life. I experienced healing in a shorter period of time than some people who have lived through the same things I have. Inner healing counseling has prepared me for what God has for me to do, at least right now, in my life.

After three and a half years of being counseled myself, I found it natural to be able to do the same inner healing counseling for others. But I still needed to take courses to learn more about what I felt led to do. Beside the classes I took, a pastor/psychologist friend allowed me to come into his practice and learn from him as he mentored me. That provided a way for me to practice my techniques while knowing I had a backup if I messed up.

Many of the classes I took, I would take more than once and would wind up teaching that class at some point. As I did more counseling and teaching, the giftings (strengths) God gave me increased. My own techniques improved. Though I didn't advertise or charge, God developed a great prayer ministry of counseling for women, through me.

My personal past experiences were a help to others in ways I never imagined. Early in our counseling relationship, I tell my clients about what I had lived through in detail. Finding out that I experienced times of disaster in my life helped my clients to feel more at ease.

As a result, when it came time for them to share something embarrassing about themselves, they felt freer to do so. They told me they knew because of what I had been willing to share with them, I would not judge them negatively. They felt more comfortable about what they needed to confess. The heavy loads they had been carrying for years were able to be taken off their backs. It allowed them to heal from their past. They understood they could find the freedom they now saw in me.

As an example, one day I was talking with a seventy-ish-year-old ex-Amish woman. She shared with me something she had not shared with anyone else. She felt she would never share this incident with anyone in her life time. Her Amish father had made her do unspeakable things with their family dog. This is called bestiality.

Once she shared that, we worked through the guilt, shame, and forgiveness. We achieved freedom for her through prayer to our heavenly Father. Then we spent time in discussion about many things afterward. She cried tears of relief. The weight of all those years of guilt, shame, embarrassment, and secret keeping were no longer on her shoulders. You would have thought that God had removed terminal cancer from her body. She responded as if He told her she would now be able to live. Her joy and celebration were fantastic to see.

There were times over the many years that I would have to stop counseling others. Something would trigger me, and I would need to get back with Dee for myself. As she had told me at the beginning, there might be instances in my life when something would trigger an emotion in me that would knock me off balance again. When that happened, I might need help healing from that trigger at any given time throughout my life. She was right.

With no forethought on my part, something would be said or would happen that would set me off balance. I wouldn't understand exactly why, but some flashback would occur. I thought Dee and I had already dealt with all the flashback issues. But throughout my life, some of them might need expansion. A whole different layer to that onion needed to be peeled off.

The Lord was helping other women through me as their counselor at the time this would happen. I was honest with myself that I needed a break as a counselor to focus on myself. While Dee never told me that I should stop counseling during these setbacks, I always felt it best to stop. If I was not at my best, I did not want to make a mistake that could hurt someone else in their healing process

Emotions take their toll on everyone. When we are emotionally charged, it is difficult to translate what God is trying to say to us. It is hard at times to figure things out for yourself. It takes an unemotionally affected spirit from someone else to help get things out in the open. It is important to expose the truths of the experience that that emotionally charged person has lived through. Even being a counselor by trade, it is hard for me to see things in perspective when I am reliving the emotionally abusive times again. That's when I need Dee to be involved.

I have spent time as the counselor and time as the one who needed to be counseled. These experiences helped me to help others to heal and find freedom from their past. Each time I experienced additional healing myself, my ladies would benefit. Somehow when I returned to counseling others, I would be able to go deeper with them. There were instances when I would experience skills as a counselor that I did not have before I took the time off to heal myself first.

The Lord frequently blows my mind with how He works. He might reveal something during my own sessions with Dee that made my life change for the better. Or He would reveal something to a client that would blow both our minds and help with the healing process. How does He know what I need to see or respond to at that particular time?

In sessions with my ladies, He might cue me to ask her a specific question. I have no forethought about that question before it comes out of my mouth. That question would provide her with a truth she needs to hear to remember something from her past. How does He know what question to feed me to ask my lady at that moment?

Often God reveals something a person needs to remember. Sometimes it is something he or she needs to understand in a different way than he or she remembered it to be. He does that to help a lady to find healing from a particular emotion or memory. She might be astonished by the results of the healing she feels from viewing that incident in another light. It isn't unusual for a husband to see a great change in his wife and ask what happened. Sometimes the husband asks for help for himself because of the affect he is seeing in his wife.

My Faith

Many of us, male and female alike, have asked, "Why am I here on earth? What is my calling/destiny or reason for being alive? Why did God put me here? Am I making any difference in the world?"

Some of us have figured out what we are here to do, at least right now, and are functioning in those roles. Many are still unsure about why God has them here. Still others, not only know what they are supposed to be doing but they also know exactly what others should be doing. Those prophetic people often share their knowledge when the time is right.

It's not uncommon for any of us, including myself, to think we have God and the world all figured out. "If only God would make this happen, all would be well!"

My family's nickname for me as a little child was "the little general." Early in my Christian walk, I would try to lead God in the direction I felt I should go. Not only did I pull God along with me, but at times I took us in the wrong direction. While I am better at following than I used to be, it's still something I must work on.

The wonderful thing is God can use us even when we are not perfect. If we are continuing to work on God's plan for us, He will use us as He molds us into His creation.

Our family did things backward from most families. Usually the parents' guide their children to the Lord. My adult sons were the guides for me in our family. I became a single mother about the time my sons were two and three years old. Working as a nurse full time, I was trying to keep up financially and physically with our lives. Trying to support my two sons and myself on a single income made finances very tight.

At that time, I was not going to church or walking with God in any form other than an occasional prayer. Even though I was not walking with God at that time, He provided all that was needed for my sons and for me. In later years, my sons and I would look back and see God in various situations. Because we were not walking with Him, we did not recognize what God was doing in our lives at the time. It was only after we were saved that we marveled at God's involvement in our past.

While God had knocked on my door many times, it seems my spirit was stubborn (stiff-necked!), deaf, and disobedient. I didn't have the energy or time to get more active with God. I couldn't take on one more re-sponsibility. At least that was my thinking at the time. I was barely able to hold our lives together as it was.

Now I know how much easier our lives would have been with Him in it. I was too stressed to figure that out on my own. And there was no one in my life lead-ing me to Christ. The decision not to include God in our lives was one of the worst decisions I ever made.

We were not going to church. None of my friends or relatives were active in a church. I had no idea what the words "to be saved" meant. It is such an easy thing to do. Much later in life I learned that being saved meant that you have asked God to take over your life. A simple prayer, just a short chat with God, and He comes into your heart and spirit. Your life is changed forever for the best. (See page 205 for more information on becoming saved.)

When the boys would visit their father, who lived out of town, they would go to church with him. My sons got saved at the same time. They were late in high school age for one of them and early in college age for the other. I watched them marry Christian women and start to raise my grandbabies in God's presence. I wanted their peace and their lives.

I was living with a man for fifteen years whom I loved dearly but never married. Early in that relationship, I developed neuropathy in my hands and feet. It is a nondiabetic neuropathy that became very painful. It was impossible for me to go to the grocery store for milk and bread without using an electric scooter. I was in so much pain I got to the point of being unable to do very little physically.

At one point I began to have words repeatedly rattle around in my head, *I don't know how much longer I can live like this. I don't know how much longer I can live like this.*

Those word were repeated over and over inside my head. I could be outside with my dog and I would hear it. I could be inside taking a shower, and I would hear it. I thought it had to do with my neuropathy. Wrong!

It turned out to be God tapping me on the shoulder harder to tell me it had to do with living without Him. "I don't know how much longer I can live like this," translated meant, "I don't know how much longer I can live without God." It took me a little while to figure that out. I knew I needed to get back to church. It took me a whole summer of church-hopping to find the right church.

I was in my early fifties before I got saved. After

taking a "Welcome to our Church" class, I asked to meet with one of the pastors. I wanted to ask him the hard questions. "Why, if there is a God, are there people starving? Why do bad things happen to good people? How can the Bible be accurate?"

While he helped me with those questions, I was still unwilling to pray the prayer used to bring God into my life. It was the prayer that would allow me to become saved.

The pastor told me he didn't want me to pray that prayer to please him. He told me God would bring a feeling to my spirit when the time was right to pray *the* prayer. He gave me a booklet and some literature, and we made another appointment for two weeks.

To my surprise, on my way home, driving on the bypass, God's spirit grabbed me. I had to pull my car off to the side of the road. Right there, right then, I had to pray the prayer to ask God to take charge of my life.

When the pastor had told me that God would provide a time in my spirit to pray this, I had no idea what he was talking about. Yet when it happened, there was no doubt in my mind what was happening. I got saved on a Friday the thirteenth in December of 2002. I could deliver a very special Christmas present to my sons and families who had been praying for this to happen for a long time.

I thought becoming saved was the end to my faith story. I'm saved now, so I will just sit back and *be* a Christian. As many of us find out, it is only the beginning. God had me in the fast lane of a learning curve when it came to my serving as a Christian woman. It became evident to me and to others that I was growing in Christ faster than most. God was using me in places that were unusual situations for a baby Christian to serve. The outcomes or the fruits of my experiences spoke for themselves.

My "crisis of faith stage," as I called it, came when I had been a Christian for less than two years. It was still early in my fight to get rid of the old woman and bring in the new woman. I was still living with the same man I eventually spent fifteen years with, hoping to bring him to Christ.

Therefore, if anyone is in Christ, he is a new creation: the old has gone, the new has come! (2 Corinthians 5:17)

The man I had been living with for fifteen years and my eighty-two-year-old father died within six months of each other. I spent at least a year and a half living the ugly part of dealing with all the legal and emotional disasters of handling two estates. When things got ugly, I would watch those negatives become trumped, one by one, with the blessings and miracles offered up from God through His grace and mercy.

I had only been saved a little under two years, and this was the first time I truly saw God in action. This time in my life became a great "learning what God can do" phase. I learned what happens when you decide to do things in your own timing without taking them to God. Then watched how things work out when you do take things to Him. When you follow His directions and timing, wonderful things happen.

As an example, I had two cars to sell. I tried to sell the first one when I became too impatient and thought things were taking too long to happen. I sold it. However, it kept coming back to haunt me for months after the sale. I learned my lesson. It took little convincing to put the second car in God's hands. What a difference in the outcome. Things just fell into place without much effort on my part. All the transactions worked out to only good things for me.

God was involved in the entire ending to a very difficult time. All the other things, when going to God first, worked out to be what was the best for me. I moved to the town where both sons and families lived. I could harass my sons and grandchildren daily. It did surprise me how many of my saved and unsaved friends and family watched my journey through all of it. They saw and commented about how going to church changed my life. Going to church helped but accepting God into my life was the key.

As I continued to grow in Christ, I found out that peace, joy, and freedom looked good on me! All that I had lived through and all that God had done gave me a way to talk about Him to others without sounding like I was shoving God down their throats. My stories, my testimonies, gave real examples of God's goodness.

The word *testimony*, like the word *saved*, always seemed confusing to me. When people talked about having a testimony, I had no idea what they were talking about. When I would hear others' testimony, it sounded like a story to me. I was listening to their story. The word *story* made it all clearer. When my story included God, it became called a testimony.

I am a chocoholic! Give me anything chocolate and my world gets better. (Except for maybe my weight!) So, did my life improve with God in it? God and chocolate cake became a fun theme in my life as I talked to more and more people about my life in Christ.

Over the years I have been able to find a friendship with God that portrays my daily existence with Him. He lives inside of me in the role of Holy Spirit. When I talk to myself I am talking to Him. Out loud, I want to sing His praises. "Thank You, Lord, for this great day. Thank You for showing me that mother goose sitting on her nest amid the rocks surrounding the pond. What a beautiful world You have created. Thank You, Lord, that while I crunched my fender into the cement planter, no one was hurt, and my car was still drivable."

Jonathan Cahn, leader of Hope of the Word Ministries and author of various books including *The Harbinger*, has another book titled *The Book of Mysteries*. He talks about the significance of one of God's names, "I Am."[6] This except from the book held great meaning to me.

> "When you speak of yourself, you say the Name." (Teacher speaking)

> "I don't understand." (Student speaking)

> "When you feel happy, you say, '*I am* happy.' And when you're not, you say '*I am* sad.' When you tell others who you are, you say, 'I am' followed by your name.

> "YHVH means 'I Am.' It's the Name of the Eternal, the Name of God. His Name is I *AM*.

> "Then we all say His Name."

---

[6] Cahn, Jonathan, *The Book of Mysteries* (Lake Mary, FL: Charisma Media, 2016), 2.

"Yes. And you have always said it. It is woven into the fabric of existence that when you speak of yourself, you must say His Name."

"Why is that?"

"It's because your existence comes from His existence. He is the I Am of all existence ... the I Am of all I ams. Your *I am* only exists because of His *I AM*. And as you exist from Him, so it is only from Him that you can find the reason and purpose of your existence. Therefore, when you say your name, you must always speak His Name. And you must always speak His Name first."

"Because ..."

"Because His existence is first and your existence flows forth from His. That's the flow of existence. Therefore, you must put Him first and then let everything flow from that. Let everything begin with Him and flow forth from Him. That's the secret of life. To not only live *for* Him, but to live your life from *Him,* to live from His living, to move from His moving, to act from His actions, to feel from His heart, to be from His being, and to become who you are from who He is ... I am."

At times He feels close, at times He feels far away, but either time He is still the great I Am. If all my efforts in all my roles are done to the best I can do and are done to please Him, my life will be more peaceful and directed.

So that boss that is driving me mad, that neighbor who is a pain, or that relative who always creates havoc in the family are not the *one* I am trying to please. They are not the *one* I want to become an obsession in my spirit and ruin my entire day.

The great I Am is the only *one*!

5

Who Am I To Talk?

For those of you who watch Joyce Meyer, you must know how hard she worked to get to be the entire ministry that is Joyce Meyer Ministry. She has often spoken about the pain, suffering, healing, and blessings it has taken to become who she is today. As a strong worker for God's kingdom, she has brought and continues to bring millions of people to the Lord. Hearing her talk about what she had to live through to get where she is today has given so many of us an ease at buying into exactly what Joyce is selling.

Joyce is selling God. In addition, she is teaching us what it is like to live day to day as a child of God. We hear almost more about her mistakes than we hear about her successes. We also hear how God used/is using those situations to her advantage as well as His advantage at the same time. She has proven herself to be someone many of us are comfortable listening to and believing what she tells us.

Learning to believe her has taken us time to get to know her—time to be able to learn more about who she is and who she was. By listening to stories about her life, whether successes or failures, we have come to trust that she is someone we want to hear from again. It doesn't matter if it's through her books, CDs, radio, or TV programs; we want to learn from her and enjoy ourselves in the process.

The easiest way for you to be sure of who I am in Christ is to hear some of my stories. I say I am a child of God, and I am, now. But I wasn't always this close to my Lord. Who was I? How did I get to where I am now? Why would you want to listen to me? Who am I to talk?

As far back as I can remember, I have always wanted to be a nurse. This is one childhood memory that has remained strong in my thoughts. Never, as I was growing up, did the desire to become a nurse change. At about the age of six or seven, I received a nurse play kit for Christmas. I remember going around to put Band-Aids on everyone, even visitors. Many kids change their minds several times about who they want to be when they grow up before they settle on a final decision. Not me. I kept the same profession in my head all the years I was growing up.

As with all children, my plans to become a nurse in no way included any negatives, such as sexual abuse. No one plans that as a part of their future. Some may not remember it as part of our past. Sexual abuse, as many of you know, is not an easy thing to deal with no matter what age you become aware of it. It doesn't matter if you have remembered it all your life or just figured it out in your fifties; it's a topic that puts your life in a whirl.

The bottom line is, there may be a need to figure it out at some point. There is a need to separate the truth and the lies to heal. Healing is needed to achieve release from the pain left behind by what happened to you in your past. That pain continues to affect your life in a negative way and needs to stop. Before God can use you for His kingdom, especially if you are going to help heal some of His children, there must be healing for you first.

It may be a pain that has been with you so long, you no longer recognize it as a pain. Or while you may recognize the pain, your memory of what caused the pain may not be accurate. The lies of Satan have become what you are most comfortable with or remember the easiest. Satan has pushed the truth of the situation to the background or even totally out of the picture.

Memories of my mom are of her staying in bed all day and drinking beer. She never taught me how to cook or be a wife in any way. Maybe that was because she stopped being those things when I was quite young. My aunt used to tell me how my father would help me dress and comb my curly brown hair when I was very young.

But quite young, I could pour a bottle of beer into a glass without spilling a drop. Mom taught me how to pour the beer on to the side of the glass to keep it from foaming over. I could get the head on that beer just enough above the top of the glass to look great but not spill over the top.

Dinners at night came from my grandmother after she came home from working all day in a local store. Exhausted and wanting to cook dinner as fast as possible to get to go home to her own house, she had no time to teach me to cook. Now I feel sad because I never helped her cook. It had become such a routine in my mind for her to do this, and it never occurred to me to help because she must be tired. Neither did my mother help her.

From second grade on, I was the one who got my brother and me out of bed and off to school. The first morning I needed to get cereal for our breakfast, I couldn't remember if you put the milk in first or the cereal. I did the milk first, and we had to push down all our cereal with a spoon to get it into the milk. Just like which came first the chicken or the egg, I needed the answer to which came first—the milk or the cereal.

I never understood what was going on with my mom until my time in therapy. Now I know that she was clinically depressed because she could do nothing to stop what was happening to me. I don't remember any scenes of my father trying to get her out of bed to take care of my brother and me or her doing anything but lying in bed drinking beer.

I do remember waking up some nights to yelling, screaming, and throwing things. My brother and I would huddle together in his bedroom. Either I didn't understand what they were arguing about, or I understood and forgot it. Either way I couldn't tell you a word they said during their fights. I just remember them as loud and scary.

Until my mid-fifties, though, I would have told you I had a great childhood. It's true I don't remember the good or the bad, but I never felt that my childhood was stressful in any way. My brother and I didn't talk about it until adulthood when I was in therapy. And even then, we only hit on surface topics, nothing in depth.

At the time of this writing, in my seventies, I have not shared with my brother about my sexual abuse. He has my father high on a pedestal. At least at this point, I am not willing to knock my dad off that pedestal. But the time may be coming to do this.

I have forgiven my dad and have asked God if he is in hell, please take him out of there. I have no idea what my father and grandfather lived through as children themselves that would cause them to do what they did to me.

Back to my mother. In that day, single motherhood was an impossible situation. She had no education past high school. No way to support herself and her children. Plus, Pappy was a very strong patriarch. I can see now where he would have come after my brother and me to bring us home. Mom felt defeated before she got out of bed each day. So why get up?

It also explains why when both my brother and I were in high school, she ran off with a married man. I hadn't seen her in years. One day I was standing in line at a drug store. She came and stood behind me in line. I was so unsure of what to do that I did nothing. When it was my turn, I paid and left. Did she know who I was and decided to react the same way I did? Or didn't she know her own daughter?

For years and years, I hated my mom for being who she wasn't. She did not do her duties as a mom as far as I was concerned. She didn't love us enough to get out of bed and get our breakfast. The lies of the enemy were strong in my mind. Condemnation does not come from God but from Satan.

During my years of therapy, I learned the truth of the situation. Mom was clinically depressed because she could not save her daughter. She knew what was happening to me. It wasn't that she did nothing to save me; she could do nothing to save me. All those years of hating her along with the pain of feeling she did not love me were wiped away in one session with Dee. I could reject Satan's lies and replace them with God's truth of the situation.

As mentioned earlier, in my mid-fifties, I took various classes geared for counselors. With no conscious effort on my part, flashbacks of my life as a child often became a part of those classes. A certain topic on certain nights would trigger thoughts in my mind while I sat in class. At first, I didn't understand what was happening. I thought only soldiers got flashbacks, PTSD. Never for a second did I consider that I was living with that process myself.

Since I'd had various types of patients as a nurse, I was familiar with the terms *amnesia, selective amnesia,* and *PTSD.* Those were situations my patients were dealing with, and as a nurse, I was trained to help them. I was not trained to accept those diagnoses as part of my life.

Life was good now. It was better than it had been in a long time. My sons were out on their own, married with children, and following God. My finances were improving, and I was in a less-stressful lifestyle.

So, what was wrong with me? Why was I having these flashbacks now? Why was I having them at all? What could be the reason behind these flashbacks? Was I seeking attention for some reason?

I lived with these flashbacks for a month or so, hoping they would go away. They did not. The longer they persisted, the worse they got. I was having problems concentrating during my classes. In each class, I was anxiously waiting for another flashback to interfere. My anxiety made it impossible for me to concentrate. It became obvious that I had to do something about them.

As a part of the program I was in to learn how to do inner healing counseling, I spent time with a counselor named Dee. Since I knew her and liked her, I decided to go to her as a client. She listened carefully while I told her what was happening to me. I explained that I had come to see her to figure out why I was making up these lies in my head. They were not my life. I didn't live what I was seeing. I was never sexually abused. These couldn't be real! She did not correct me.

While it took me a while to get out of the denial stage, once I was out of it, certain things fell into place or made sense to me. There were things from my past that had always been questions in my mind—for instance, how I had fallen asleep each night for as long as I could remember.

I would be awake and start the process as a daydream. While awake with my eyes closed, I would imagine myself being tied up some way and being tortured. Fighting the ropes, I was trying to free myself. The imaginary me would be exhausted and so hurting that fighting to escape the bounds was nearly impossible. But someone would come to my rescue each night. It was always someone who loved me, as in a boyfriend or husband. If I had a boyfriend at the time, that person would be him. When I didn't have a boyfriend, my rescuer would be a faceless male. Each night I would drift off to sleep while the imaginary man who loved me would be sitting by my hospital bed holding my hand as I was recovering. I was free. I was safe.

Since I did not realize that I was sexually abused until my mid-fifties, I could not understand why I would run the same scenario repeatedly each night in order to fall asleep. I did this as a child and well into my adulthood. I don't need those scenarios anymore.

Little did I know that it would take three and a half years of counseling to answer all these questions. Those years would be spent looking at my entire childhood and would totally change my idea of who I was. Those I loved became people I didn't know at all. How could all of this happen, and I not remember any of it until now? Nurse Darci knew the answer to that question, but wounded Darci had a lot to learn before she could answer that question.

With Dee and I doing the same type of counseling, I want to mention one more thing about how this works. I want you to understand that *I* eventually told Dee about my abuse. She did not tell me. When I finally told one of my sons about my sexual abuse, his first question was important: "Who told you that you were sexually abused? Did a counselor talk you into it?"

His concern was that someone, maybe with the best intentions, made a wrong diagnosis. My son was concerned that a therapist labeled me something that I was not. It was just as hard for him to believe as it was for me to believe. In fact, I did not feel led to tell him until after I had completed my counseling with Dee. I was led to tell my sons one on one and as it turned out a few years apart. I allowed the Lord to lead me to when, where, and exactly what to say.

Inner healing is done between God and whomever needs healing. Both Dee and I, as counselors, are really intercessors. Intercessors pray to God on behalf of someone else. Our jobs are really to help our clients connect to God, interpret what God is telling them, and protect them. If the client needs help figuring something out and gets stuck, often God will feed Dee or me a question to ask our client. Speaking for myself, every time God does that, what He has put into my head has turned out to be the key to opening my client's mind. God is the Ultimate Counselor.

Neither Dee nor I tell our clients that they have been abused in any way or about anything that is traumatic to their lives. As in my case, as a client of Dee's, I was the one to tell her I was sexually abused. God gave me a picture in my head of what my grandfather was doing to me. He showed me my grandfather's actions first. Many sessions later, He revealed what my father had done to me.

God determines the time and place for a client to learn something life altering. Anyone who does inner healing appropriately allows God to lead. Often the counselor has already figured out what God will be revealing but keeps it to herself. The counselor guides the client through whatever God is revealing to him or her.

As protectors, we counselors have learned ways to tell if what the client is saying is true or false. Has the devil spoken instead of God? We make sure, through various ways, that only our Creator is the counselor. The last thing our clients need is additional pain and interference.

My son who asked that question does prayer ministry with people in his church. Therefore, he understood what I was telling him about my time with Dee. God is the Great Healer. Dee and I are guides, supporters, protectors, and interpreters who also hear from God during the session and obey His leading. With practice, most counselors know what the issues are before God reveals them. But still, we do not tell them what we feel will come out in further sessions.

One of my clients who had been dancing around the topic of sexual abuse for several sessions finally said to me, "I think it's time to stop these sessions. I have worked hard to push my past out of the way. It took me a long time to take control of things, and I have no desire to do anything about my past."

While I was disappointed for her, as in all cases, the client has the control to stop things at any time. As years went on, I watched this client date a pastor, try to be a missionary, and be unable to settle peacefully into God's plan for her. All these situations failed to produce good fruit. God cannot allow anyone who is not healed themselves to help some of His other hurting children. He does not want us hurting others because we ourselves are still hurting enough to injure others instead of helping them.

> Blessed be the God and Father of our Lord Jesus Christ, the Father of mercies and God of all comfort, who comforts us in all our tribulations, that we may be able to comfort those who are in any trouble, with the comfort with which we ourselves are comforted by God. For as the sufferings of Christ abound in us, so our consolation also abounds through Christ. (2 Corinthians 1:3–5 NKJV)

Each week, with God leading, Dee helped me to explore my past. While Dee knew early on that I was a sexual abuse victim, she never revealed it to me. This is why I spent my first three months in therapy in the denial stage. I had little memory about my childhood, good or bad, so I continued to consciously deny what my subconscious already knew.

One session something happened inside my brain.

I started telling Dee what I now saw in my mind's eye. Out loud I was acknowledging that I remembered my grandfather sexually abusing me. Finally, the healing would be able to begin.

Those three months in denial were not a waste of my time. There were some things God had revealed during that denial time that helped me to accept the truth. God used that time for preparation. Once His preparation was complete, He moved me on to healing. He is the one who put memories in my brain for me to finally recall after all these years of lost family history.

As the scenes kept coming during my sessions, occasionally I would ask Dee if she was sure I was not making this up. I knew what I was seeing in my head but couldn't totally accept them as real. She shared with me why she knew that I was not making the scenes up.

Dee explained that she had been doing counseling for eleven years. There were ways she could know who was telling the truth about their abusive past and who was lying. I learned that watching body language was one of those ways to tell who was telling the truth.

My eyes would be closed during our sessions, so I was not aware that Dee was watching my nonverbal reactions to the scenes I would tell her about. As I told the story about what I saw in my head, unknown by me, I would move myself in the chair in a way to try to protect myself. I would automatically physically move myself to protect certain parts of my body as they fit into the scene I was recalling.

Dee had explained, and I knew that I was safe in her office. No one was going to hurt me. But when I would recount the past scene to her, it would feel so real to me that I would move to protect myself. God would pick a memory to show me in my mind's eye. While I was talking, I was also reacting. I never felt myself move. It felt to me like I was sitting still in my chair the entire session. I had no idea until Dee revealed it to me of what I had been doing each week for protection.

Now, as a counselor myself, I have seen some of my clients do the same thing. Like Dee, I have learned to observe the nonverbal communications. Most times, the nonverbal reactions are truer reactions to what God is showing my client than the verbal response to the session.

There are times when clients are unwilling to share what they are really seeing in their heads. They feel shame, guilt, or embarrassment to the point of wanting to keep what they are seeing to themselves. As with me when I was the client, the nonverbal actions reveal the truth of what they are feeling. Even if we as counselors don't know what they are seeing in their scene, we can deal with the emotions they are projecting.

Some of my nonverbal reactions were dramatic. With no forethought on my part, I would drop to the floor to lie there in the fetal position, shaking all over. My hands would fly down between my tightly crossed legs to try to protect myself in that area. Those nonverbal responses, which physically took me out of my chair, I would feel, as opposed to the lesser movement while sitting in my chair that I would not feel.

The movement to the floor reactions were too dynamic for me to miss. Dee kept a pillow and blanket in her office always. I learned to carry a candy bar in my purse. Some of these types of sessions were so intense, I would have to get some sugar in me before Dee would allow me to drive home.

The exhaustion of dealing with a session like this was debilitating. It was physical enough for me to need to replace my energy with something heavy with sugar. A Milky Way bar was my sugar of choice at the time. It also allowed me to feel like I was rewarding myself for all the hard work that took place during these sessions. Chocolate and God to the rescue!

"I see a ring on a finger. A man's ring on a man's hand," I said hesitantly.

I was talking out loud. While inside my head, I was questioning where that vision came from—questioning why I would say such a thing. What did it mean?

This was one of the first memories while with Dee to flash back before my eyes, so to speak, since my eyes were closed. While I had had flashbacks in my classroom, this was the first time with Dee present. This is the beginning of a long battle with flashbacks as part of my healing time in therapy.

Over the three and a half years, these memories would take me on a trek from the pits of hell to the heights of freedom and joy! Memories I had long forgotten, or maybe never consciously remembered, would start to come back now. This, for me, was a new discovery, this vision of that ring. I managed to continue.

"I see a gold ring with an insignia on it. It's on the ring finger of his right hand." I'm trying to give Dee more information about what I am seeing. At the same time, I am trying to convince myself that I am not making this up.

"A thick gold ring with a black center and a gold etching on top of the black center." I continued in my description. It reminded me of a high school class ring, yet somehow, I knew it had nothing to do with a class ring. As I viewed this ring, I felt sick to my stomach, depressed, and in a dark place all at the same time.

After some hesitation, I started telling Dee a story. "There was a man who lived in the attic of my grandparents' house while they were alive. His name was Eric," I explained to Dee, trying to keep my eyes closed so I could see it better.

"The ring is on the ring finger of his right hand," I repeated, trying to confirm to myself that I was seeing all this in my mind's eye. I'd forgotten all about Eric. It was a long, long time ago. In my memory bank, it was as if he had not existed in my life until now.

"Can you see what's on the ring?" asked Dee. "Maybe start with other colors, if that helps."

I squeezed my eyes shut tighter, willing my brain to see it clearer. "It has a black background with a drawing on it in the same gold color as the ring itself."

"Do you recognize the drawing?" asked Dee.

"I've seen it before, but I don't know what it means," I said, sitting back in my chair to get more comfortable. This session had turned into one of the longest I'd had with Dee so far. "It's hard to explain," I continued.

"How about drawing it for me? Do you think you can do that?" Dee asked.

"Yes, I think I could do that. Is it okay to open my eyes now?" Dee liked me to keep my eyes closed for most sessions. When one of your senses is shut down, the other senses get stronger.

"Yes, open your eyes. We're going to do some research," explained Dee as she handed me a piece of paper and a pen.

I drew what I was seeing, sketching it rapidly. It was as clear to me as if Eric were standing in front of me at that moment showing me his ring, which he never did—that I remember. I wondered why I could see it so clearly now. Plus, Eric was only in my life for a few years. Those years were when I was eight or ten years old.

"I have few memories of him except seeing him come down the steps from the attic all clean and neat, heading out to go somewhere. He is the same age as my grandparents. Yet his walk has a younger step to it even though he is very bowlegged. He always smiled at me and said hello as he passed by me on his way out the door," I told Dee as that memory flowed through my brain.

"Hmmm," Dee said, taking the piece of paper and the pen from me. "It sort of looks familiar to me too. But I couldn't tell you either what it means. Let's get into the computer and look around."

We both stood up and moved around to the other side of Dee's desk. She sat at the computer, and I stood looking over her right shoulder. "Wow, just what I love, a mystery!" I said, sounding more jovial than I felt.

I would find out, over time, just how big and involved this mystery was going to be. I had no idea how important it would be as a part of my healing process. The mystery would bring back the memory I needed from my past to find healing in the present, all of which will influence a healthier future. It was a mystery that would continue to show itself at times for the rest of my life.

"It looks like they have insignias for everything," I offered.

"This could take a bit. There are lots of them," I said, feeling a little disappointed.

Dee skimmed through the pictures. To my surprise, in very little time we hit pay dirt. "There it is," she said.

"That was quick," I said. "I expected it to take longer. It must be pretty popular to be at the beginning of all these pictures."

"It says that this insignia is the insignia for a specific cult," Dee read off the screen. "Does that mean anything to you?" She looked up to me in search of an answer to her question.

"Well, I know that my family belonged to a group that met together, but I did not consider it a cult. All my family, including aunts, uncles, parents, and grandparents, belonged to some form of this group. My brother belonged to a group made up of younger men or boys. My mom belonged to a part of the group that included the wives only. The group my dad belonged to was for men over the age of twenty-one. I belonged to the group of girls under twenty-one. About all I remember is going to some dances they had for the boys' group and the girls' group together."

As I moved back to my chair, Dee continued to skim other rings just to be sure of what she had found. It was not long until she returned to her seat too. During that time of waiting for her to return to her seat, I was quietly searching my memory of my past, surprised at how little I remembered.

I need to interject a note here. When I was in my late teens or early twenties, Eric died. To my shock, he left me his very large, beautiful family Bible that listed his family over several generations. The Bible itself was written entirely in German. He also left to me a small antique chest filled with smaller, very old Bibles.

I could never understand why he did that. He

represented a nice man to me but not someone I knew well. It was only years later at the end of my therapy sessions that I think I understood. He was part of the group of men who had raped me as part of a satanic ritual, as explained in the section on satanic cults. I can only guess that he felt guilty being part of that group. Somehow, he must have felt by giving me these family Bibles, he was making things right.

How do you know when you have truly forgiven someone? When you sit here writing about him with tears in your eyes, hurting for him. I can't imagine the pain from the guilt he must have had in his heart as he faced his own death. He had to be alone, with no family or close friends. How alone he must have felt to decide to give me his family treasures. I truly hurt in my heart at his memory now that I know more about my past.

A few weeks later in this healing therapy process with Dee, I experienced a confirmation of my past. This confirmation helped me to verify what I was seeing truly happened to me. Throughout my time with Dee, often if I was finding myself in doubt over something, God would provide a partial memory that helped me to find peace.

That partial memory would explain something I might have bouncing around in my head. Or it might answer a question I had in my mind about something I half remembered from long ago. For example: Why have I, over the years even as an adult, had frequent dreams of my closet in my childhood bedroom?

Later, I would recall that at the age of five, my father would tie me up nude and put me in my closet. I was so scared in the dark, and the ropes hurt. I would sing "Jesus Loves Me" to keep myself brave. Jesus would come and be with me in that closet. We would sing together.

The strangest part of this memory was that while my dad did things that should have left me with nightmares, I had good feelings about that closet. Once I was shown that Jesus came and sang with me, I could understand why a bad situation left behind good feelings.

As a child growing up with my grandfather, Pappy, I knew him as a tall, balding man with short white hair circling around the back of his head from ear to ear. Yet when the memories were coming to me showing the abusive situations as they occurred, I saw him with some dark hair over most of his head.

One day while going through some old photos, I found a picture of my grandparents when they were younger. He had the exact hair situation in that picture that I was seeing in my memories provided by God. I had not, to my knowledge, seen any pictures of him as a younger man that I could remember. This was the first picture of him that I could see him with hair, not balding.

There is no way I could have put that picture of my younger grandfather in my head, unless I had seen him with dark hair on his head. This was one of the first confirmations over the years of therapy that God sent me to help me realize that I was not making this all up.

At the time, I was having trouble believing Dee when it came to this theory of my not making it all up. Though I trusted her with so many other things I shared with her, I had thought she was just telling me I was not making these things up just to be an agreeable person.

In life, there are many "morning afters." Mine was the morning after finally experiencing a late-night, eye-opening session with Dee. Trying to get out of bed and start my day was difficult. This session had made it possible for me to totally leave the denial stage and move on. It was one of the first sessions in which I truly accepted that my flashbacks were the real story of my life.

I was sitting on the edge of my bed trying to wake up. Sleeping is an escape mechanism I often use when overwhelmed. Plus, I was exhausted from the in-depth session the night before. So even though I had been overwhelmed and was in shock about what my session had revealed, falling asleep that night was quite easy.

On my way home from the session, I thought I would have trouble falling asleep. I was very keyed up, and since it was later at night than I usually get home from my sessions, there was a shorter time to come down before trying to sleep.

It surprised me the next morning when I realized that as soon as I got home and hit the bed, I was asleep. It was the waking up part that was more difficult than the falling asleep part. I was waking up later than usual on that Saturday morning, which in my mind made me think I should feel rested. But it was still very difficult to clear my head, and I felt groggy. Trying hard to clear my head by shaking it, I heard myself say out loud, "Oh, now I remember," mumbling incoherently.

"Last night my world was turned upside down. Who am I, really? My family, who were they? Now what do I do? How do I act? Do I go about life the same? Do I go to my conference today?" It was hard not to just fall back into bed. I knew I wouldn't sleep.

My head was swimming. Confusion, doubt, rejection, hurt, you name it. All the negative emotions that the enemy could throw at me were in my head. I felt really weighted down and totally off balance. While I am usually a confident person, I was unsure of everything except where my next breath was coming from. My next breath comes from my Lord, so I needed to hear from my God to get the answer to my question, "Now what do I do?"

I still had not moved from the edge of my bed. I prayed out loud to my Savior, my Deliverer. "God, help me. I am so lost and confused. What do I do next? How do I get out of this bed and move on? It's Saturday morning, and I have a seminar to go to today. Do I go? Do I stay home? Help!"

If I wouldn't have had to pee as badly as I had to, I probably would have rolled right back into bed. But God provides always—even with something as basic as the urge to empty my bladder, which would make me move ahead. At least I was up and moving. Temporarily.

I sat back on the edge of my bed after leaving the bathroom. As if the Lord was sitting right beside me on the edge of my bed, I heard in my left ear, "Yes, you do go to the seminar. Your weekend is full for a reason. I planned it this way. All of this is part of My plan for you. Follow My schedule as I have already laid it out to you for the weekend. Just keep putting one foot in front of the other."

My head was still spinning. Even with God adding His response so prominently, quickly, and directly, I felt I needed to keep praying. If I stood up now, I was not sure that my legs would hold me.

I prayed something like this, "God, I thank You

for giving me this clear direction. Help me to concentrate on what You want me to hear and do this
weekend. I give all of me and all this situation to You.
I place what is happening to me before You for You to
control. Help me to continue to hear and obey Your
minute-by-minute instruction to my day. I submit myself to the calling You have on my life and the healing
I need to do to accomplish each task. I love You, Lord.
Amen"

I went to the seminar, and to my amazement, I
could concentrate, talk somewhat intelligently, and receive what I was to get out of the seminar. Amazingly,
as hurt as I was, I did not have a twinge of need to
stand up and tell everyone what had happened to me
last night.

I realize I am not exactly the norm! You must understand more of who I am. I am just as comfortable
standing up in front of a large group of people and
talking openly to them as I am sitting on the couch
talking openly to my best friend. God gave me a mouth
that runs away with itself easily.

I have the strong desire to teach others. When I
have learned something I feel will help someone else, I
am quick to share. Good or bad, I can verbally expose
my own emotions with comfort. That is because I know
others feel like this too at times but don't express it
openly. Someone needs to talk about these things out
loud. In addition, somehow God gave me the ability
to quickly make large groups of people my immediate
friends. But not that weekend.

I responded to the leader of the seminar when appropriate, and I spoke when spoken to one on one. I
answered in front of the thirty others only when it was
my turn, staying on topic. Surprisingly, I absorbed

what was coming to me through that preplanned seminar that God had already put on my schedule.

I also remember sitting by a friend as the presenter talked about SRA. I asked my friend what those initials stood for. He told me. Little did I know that I had experienced satanic ritual abuse and would be learning about it firsthand in the near future.

It still felt like the weirdest day I had ever had. At times, it felt like I didn't know for sure who I was any more. I wasn't sure how to respond to many of the normal situations of the day. In some ways, I was almost detached from myself. But I was alert enough to fake it. And while I was moving, I felt like I was moving slowly through a mud screen ahead of me. It felt like my motions were produced in slow motion to the world.

I never thought, years later, to go back to some of the people at the seminar who know me well to see if they noticed a difference in me. It would have been interesting to hear their thoughts.

Not long after that weekend of dealing with what was truly my reality, God decided it was time to begin the really hard work. One of my weekly sessions with Dee became intense and all too real rather quickly. I no longer had my denial to use as a defense shield to keep the truth out.

God showed me my Pappy, my grandfather, and the house he and my Mimi lived in. Pappy and I were upstairs in one of the bedrooms. I was about three years old in the scene God put before me through my mind's eye. As an adult Darci sitting in the chair in Dee's office, my eyes were closed, but the scene with the three-year-old me was as clear as watching a movie or TV show.

Dee told me as she saw me tensing up, "Darci, it's okay whatever you're seeing. You are safe. No one will hurt you here. Be sure to tell me all the things you are hearing and seeing. I need to know what you know."

"I see my Pappy standing beside the bed. I see myself lying on top of the bed as a three-year-old, and I don't have any clothes on," I explained to Dee.

"Darci." Dee was speaking softly but directly to what I needed to do. "You need to watch this scene. Even if it gets uncomfortable or scary, you need to let me know what is happening. You are safe here. No one is going to hurt you. No one is going to touch you. But I need to hear what you are being shown."

"Okay, I'll try." I swallowed the lump in my throat before I went on. "Pappy is moving toward me, and he has a coat hanger repositioned, sort of straightened out and doubled back on itself a couple of times. It is in his right hand." This time I felt myself change my position in my chair.

Later Dee explained to me that I moved to protect myself between my legs by crossing my legs as tightly as I could and reaching down with my hands to protect that area between my legs.

"Remember, no one is going to hurt you now. But keep watching to see what happens, and try not to shut down the scene," Dee reminded me. She prayed, "Lord, allow Darci to see what You want her to see but not to experience the pain or other physical discomforts of this scene."

I continued explaining to Dee as the scene revealed itself. "My Pappy is trying to keep me from crying or moving or closing my spread-out legs. He's positioning me on the bed with my legs spread out and my head and my arms off to the side. Every time I close my legs or cry or don't allow myself to remain spread open on the bed, he whips me between my legs with the reshaped clothes hanger."

I understand somehow but don't feel that the pain is almost more than I can stand in the scene. Mercifully, I do not feel that pain now as the adult Darci telling Dee what's happening to the three-year-old Darci.

Right now, sitting here writing this, I get a squeamish feeling in the pit of my stomach. I find myself changing my position on the chair I am sitting on. This is not easy to relive.

Weeping gently, I told Dee, "I think I am being trained to allow men to use me sexually without me crying, moving, or fighting them off. I am supposed to lay like this no matter what is done to me and no matter who is doing it to me."

How I knew that, I don't know. I could only guess that my grandfather had explained that to me and somehow as a three-year-old, I understood what I was to do and not do. Later that night once I got home, I reviewed those scenes in my head. I found myself wondering, *Why would a grandfather who is supposed to love and protect you do something like that?*

As the days went on after that session, I realized some other facts relating to this story. It became clear to me that as a child I had been sexually abused by a group of nude men with hoods on. I found out that if I resisted the man on top of me, I would suffer a worse fate from my pappy than that sexual abuse.

I knew if I did not lay still like trained to do in that upstairs bedroom, he would whip me between my legs with that redesigned coat hanger on a later date as a reminder. He wanted to be sure that I would do a better job next time. The pain from the whipping was so severe that allowing myself to be sexually abused by a group of nude, fat, dirty old men in hoods was far better than the alternative.

The scene from that session of my grandfather training me was winding down with a little more from that bedroom upstairs. Dee was speaking to me, the adult Darci, as I was telling the story of the three-year-old me. "What's happening now, Darci?"

"I am still laying spread eagle on the bed, not crying, not moving, allowing my pappy to do what he wants to me," I explained. "The training has been a success. My Pappy is pleased. I am dead. I am no longer crying. I am not moving"

As the scene faded away, the adult me became focused on the thoughts and feelings of that three-year-old. "Pappy is finished and gets off the top of me," I continued to tell Dee.

"My head is still turned to the left, half buried in the pillow. My mind is numb. My eyes are open. Yet, the three-year-old me is focused on nothing in the bedroom. I'm still lying there spread eagle on the bed. I can't move. I have become dead inside. The child in me no longer exists.

"Every organ, every muscle, every nerve in my body no longer feels a thing. I am outside my own body, floating above myself, looking down seeing myself still as the three-year-old. But in the vision in the head of that part of me hovering over my body, I am dressed in a beautiful, frilly white dress. There are bows and ribbons flowing in the gentle breeze from my hair and from my dress. I am in a field of beautiful flowers, with the sun shining down on me, skipping along, humming, happy, smiling, picking the colorful flowers as I

skip along." The adult me started to cry uncontrolla-
bly, mourning for the three-year-old.

How does this happen to a three-year-old? How
can a three-year-old figure this all out in her brain?
How did I know or understand what all this meant
at the age of three? How could I continue to love my
Pappy all his life knowing he did this to me?

The answer—by not remembering any of this that
happened to me until I was in my mid-fifties. My Pappy
was dead by then. Selective amnesia allowed me to remember the good parts of my life with my pappy and
Mimi while suppressing the painful times.

As a three-year-old, I had found a way to be somewhere else. In my mind, I was no longer in the bedroom experiencing what just happened to my body.
When needed I could be in a place of beauty and
peace instead of being in the satanic cult's auditorium
surrounded by hooded men. My first part or alter or
personality outside of myself had been formed.

There are times when a situation becomes more
than someone can handle. The only way to survive it
is to go somewhere else in a made-up world that com-
pensates for the real world at least for a space of time.
On demand, even at the age of three, I could change
places within my mind. But I was always able to return to reality when it was time to do so.

The scene faded away, and I was back to the adult
Darci sitting in my chair in Dee's office. I was crying
beyond consolation for that crushed three-year-old
me. As I was sitting in Dee's office, I came to a painful
realization. It occurred to me that the rest of my childhood years, as well as my adult years up to now, were
experienced through the spirit of a child whose spirit
was killed at the age of three. At the same time that

night, I had to work to accept that that three-year-old is actually me.

Dee handed me some Kleenex without touching me. "You did great. That was extremely hard. Keep crying as long as you want to until you feel done. Take your time. Then we will talk."

She did not move to touch me or soothe me through any contact from her body to mine. Since she had been doing this for quite a while, she knew that as much as she cared and wanted to soothe me, anyone trying to touch my body right now, even as a form of comfort, would be rejected. It was imperative that no one touch me right now.

This session with my Pappy whipping me between my legs with a coat hanger was a life-altering realization. It would affect me for the rest of my life even after I healed from it. Just writing this right now, sitting safely in my office, many, many years later, my insides still curl up in a ball. I feel sick to my stomach.

Exactly how much healing have I done that I still react like this? A long time ago Dee had explained to me that for periods of time throughout the rest of my life, I will be dealing with another layer of certain situations that I lived through as a child. This is one of those times!

After this session, as I continued my normal schedule. I could be hugged by my male family members when appropriate to the situation. But this was the beginning of not knowing if I could ever let a man touch me again in any intimate way.

Never again will I allow this, kept coming into my mind repeatedly.

I will never allow another man to touch me. No man will ever hurt me again. An unhealthy vow had just been formed and at this point would not allow me to form any healthy relationships with any males other than my sons.

I would need to correct this thought process later in life. I had to consciously break off that unhealthy vow through prayer and time with my Deliverer. And while I have corrected those thoughts, not having to put that correction into actions, I wonder if I can ever physically make love again. At the time of this writing, God has not brought a husband into my life to test this theory.

Over those years of being counseled, I would recognize a pattern. I figured out that in my past, as an adult woman in a relationship as a wife or even a girlfriend, I would never be honest with the boy/man about my thoughts or feelings. When my husband or boyfriend or really any male would say that we were going here or we were going to do this, I would just say okay and submit to their wishes.

I would never say, "I'd rather do this instead" or "Let's do it later." It turns out, in these situations I was still, as an adult woman, subconsciously afraid of being beaten between my legs by my Pappy. Deep in my brain it still registered that if I spoke out and said, "I don't want to do that" or "I don't agree with that," I would be beaten between my legs with my Pappy's whip for not doing what the man wants me to do. This continued long after my Pappy had died.

It was all in my own mind and my spirit. Never once did any of these men threaten me physically or psychologically. Never once did any of them make me feel uncomfortable about voicing my opinion. Some would even ask what I wanted to do. I would say that I didn't care. This reaction was all from within me.

This was one of the things I needed to heal from to become whole. I needed to be able to say what I was thinking. I needed to not allow the enemy to bring my Pappy and the pain he inflicted into my present world. The situation with Pappy is no longer the truth of the present world I live in. This was probably the worst or one of the worst hurts from my past that was hardest to heal from completely.

The next week with Dee, we were right back into the same scene with Pappy and me upstairs in the same bedroom. But Pappy and I had moved ahead. Somehow the three-year-old me did manage to move again and get dressed. As Pappy and I descended the stairs, Mimi was waiting for us at the bottom. Instead of the sympathy I craved from my Mimi because of what I just went through, out of her mouth came something else that would affect me the rest of my life.

"My pet," Mimi always called me her pet. However, this time she was not addressing me in any soothing manner. Her voice was harsh and condemning. "My pet! Why did you make your Pappy do that to you?"

I was stunned! I was unable to respond. I only retreated further inside myself and let those words slide between my already dead muscles, joints, and brain. I did manage to add guilt to the negative emotions already swimming around inside my dead body—guilt that I did something wrong and that is why my grandfather treated me that way. I deserved that beating. My grandmother, whom I loved dearly and thought she loved me, had just added guilt to the enemies already negative emotions. In that short time, I had already taken on feelings of shame, embarrassment, hurt, and feeling equal to a piece of dirt. I was no better than a piece of dirt. No wonder no one loved me.

As a three-year-old, I couldn't deal with any of this in my mind, so I shut it all down through selective amnesia. As an adult, I still hadn't figured out any of this. I hadn't remembered any of this. I managed to go through each day of my life thinking my life was good, that my life was a normal life.

It took God to show me what it was that I needed to understand and remember. I needed to know what had happened to me as a child to heal my spirit. God decided to wait until my mid-fifties to start that process and after my dad and grandfather were dead.

God's timing is perfect. He knew I couldn't handle all that I learned in these two sessions in the same week's session. He knew He needed to separate the two weeks, the two life-altering experiences, but only by a short span of time. I had needed to be able to keep the week before fresh in my spirit. Both experiences needed to be looked at and healed from as they both tied into each other.

Part of my healing process included a trip back home for a weekend. Without any forethought, I found myself at our family cemetery plot. When I went home that weekend, I had not considered a trip to the cemetery in my conscious planning. Yet there I was, standing in the cemetery.

I walked around to remind myself who was there besides my dad and grandparents. There were two sets of aunts and uncles, along with two single uncles, brothers of my grandfather. I started to stomp my feet on the grave site of my grandparents. I was stomping and yelling at them. "Why did you do this to me? How could you treat me this way? I thought you loved me. How could you call me your pet?"

I turned around to my uncles' graves. I now knew

they had to also be a part of the satanic cult group. It was generational and active in family groups. As I was stomping on their graves, I was declaring my freedom. "You all have affected my entire life up till now. I will no longer allow you to negatively affect one more day of my life!"

Slowly I wandered back to my grandparents' graves and fell to the ground on top of them. I was crying with anger, still not understanding how they could do this to me. Then I heard from God. Just as before, He was talking into my left ear.

He explained how Mimi could call me her pet and still do what she did. In her world, the rituals of the satanic cult group were almost normal to her. Her family as well as my grandfather's family were probably involved for generations.

Later I learned that my grandfather was one of the head poo-pawhs. So, to Mimi, it was an honor to be in their position in the group. She wanted me to be the virginal sacrifice because it put our family and me in a higher position of honor and fame. In her mind, she was putting me in a place of honor, fame, and high social status. She was doing it because she loved me. She thought she was doing good.

Yes, it was wrong. Yes, it was sick to think that way. But that was how she was raised. This had been part of her life since she was a child. Maybe she was a virginal sacrifice at one time herself. Maybe it brought her fame and she wanted that fame for me.

I could stop crying and start praying. Having that information from God helped me to be able to forgive my father and grandparents when it came time to do that.

After I returned from that weekend away, God in

his infinite wisdom allowed me a few weekly sessions to come to grips with what He had shown me in the last two sessions. The next few sessions were easy and positive. God showed me only positive, happy scenes. When He felt the timing was right, He got back into it again. Just when I finally felt like I could catch my breath, He brought another heavy scene to my mind. Several weeks later, I again told Dee what was happening.

"This time God has me a large room, like an auditorium." I started to hesitantly remember the details of the last two in-depth sessions as I related the present scene to Dee.

"I am lying in the center of the large room on top of what looks like an altar. I am ten years old." I was quiet for a few seconds, and Dee gave me a chance to continue in my own timing.

"Surrounding me on all sides are large, fat, dirty old men, nude from the neck down. On their heads are white or light tan hoods. I cannot see their faces. I can only see their eyes and mouths." I stopped talking for another few moments.

I stopped talking because I couldn't tell if they were singing or talking. The noise was adding to the confusion around me as I lay on the altar. The loud chanting of many nude, hooded men as they circled me made my head spin. I felt dizzy even though I was lying down. They were all chanting the same words, but I couldn't understand what they were saying.

"I am tied spread eagle, nude, to all four corners of the altar, but I still have limited movement of my extremities on top of the altar. As all the men move in closer to me, the human circle around me makes me feel closed in. It's harder to breathe. Fear and confusion sit heavily on my chest.

"I am looking all around me as best I can, waiting to see who is going to be the first one to make a move and crawl on top of me." I hesitated to tell Dee what was going on again to watch the scene move on to the next happening. Dee still did not say a word.

"The one who starts to move first is ..." I paused here, unable to believe what I was seeing, unable to verbalize the reality. What I was seeing caused my brain and spirit to explode, as if my entire body had blown apart from the inside out, shattered into tiny pieces. I recognized those eyes.

I started talking to Dee again. "They are my father's eyes." I was barely able to talk through the crying. My voice was cracking, and tears leaked through the sleep mask I now used during my sessions with Dee to help me keep my eyes closed without thinking about it.

With my sleep mask still in place, I was still in the scene, but the scene froze as if someone yelled freeze. Everyone but me was frozen in place. In the scene, all others had stopped midmovement, except me.

I was fighting against the ropes used to tie me to the altar. I was in shock that those eyes could possibly be from my father, who was supposed to be the one to love me and protect me. I was unable to allow the scene to go any further at this stage of the session.

I was telling Dee, "The scene is frozen in place. All I can see are my father's eyes inside that hood looking down on me. I can't believe it is him. My father. Looking at me like that, lustfully? How could he be part of this horrible group? How could he not stop what was being done to me? Didn't he love me?" I was asking Dee this between my sobs and trying to suck air into my lungs at the same time.

Dee told me softly, "I know this is tremendously hard for you, but if the scene is still there, try to keep watching it for a few minutes to see if it changes or goes away." I continued to sob and kept repeating the same questions repeatedly. "How can this be my father? But I know those eyes. I know it's my father. How could he do this to me?"

With the scene still frozen, I didn't actually see my father climb on top of the ten-year-old me. But I knew somehow that that's what happened next. I mentally pushed the scene away still in that frozen image state. I was unable to continue watching that scene. I told Dee I needed to stop. I took off my sleep mask and continued to sob.

Again, Dee gave me Kleenex without touching me and encouraged me to cry as long as I needed to do that. She reassured me that we would talk when I was ready. Dee and I spent a large part of the night talking about what God had shown me. Since the scene itself did not last long, we had time to hear what God wanted us to talk about. I was still crying but able to say, "Are you sure I am not making this up? First my pappy and now my own dad?"

"Quite honestly," Dee said, "I have been waiting for this next step. Satanic cults are a generational sect. So, if your grandfather was doing this to you, I could only guess that your dad was somewhere in the mix too."

Dee was explaining this to me, speaking slowly, trying to give me time to collect myself. She also wanted to stay on the topic without really answering any of my questions just yet.

They weren't really questions to be answered anyway. It was just me talking out loud, wondering out loud. But what I had learned from this scene needed to be explored in more depth. Because I closed down the scene, Dee knew she couldn't let me go home without some more work on the topic.

Gently, she helped me explore what I had learned, what I was feeling. She explained how God was going to be involved in the whole process of what I had just learned. God would be there for me for all things I might learn as time went on. We prayed together, cried together and just hung out together.

As mentioned before, in the sessions to follow, over the three and a half years, I would learn to carry a candy bar in my purse to each session. As exhausted as I would get, sometimes I needed the sugar rush to be able to drive home. Dee would know just when it was right for me to leave, to move on. She would allow enough time with God and her to achieve whatever was to happen that evening.

Later, over time, as my sessions progressed, I would find more than one part or alter or personality was formed during those overwhelming experiences in my childhood years. Those experiences were beyond anything the ten-year-old me, or the other ages of my childhood me, could deal with without the help of that other part of me.

As mentioned in the amnesia part of this book, to deal with my earthly father's and grandfather's sexual abuse in my life, I needed to escape to a false world at times. Thankfully, as happens to some people, I did not get stuck in the make-believe world. I could come and go between escape and reality as I needed to in order to survive.

Toward the end of my three and a half years, I could find a healthy, adult Darci. I got to the place in my life where life was good again. The sun shone brighter. Colors were more distinct. I would still have some tough days, but in general more days were good than bad.

Dee and I have broken off most of the curses or negative vows I had unknowingly made throughout my childhood experiences. My parts have all integrated. I moved out of my apartment, bought a house, and am doing counseling myself.

Instead of weekly sessions, I progressed to sessions every two to three weeks. There were even occasions during my sessions when God would change the focus. I would start out being the client as usual with Dee being the counselor. Then in midsession, without either Dee or I knowing this would happen, God would change the focus. I became the counselor and Dee became the client.

Thank You, Lord, for Your timing. As a gentleman, You knew when and how much to deliver to my spirit at a time. You are the ultimate Counselor and Friend.

Finally, after ending three and a half years of therapy, Dee and I have become good friends and sisters in Christ who love God and want nothing more than to obey and do our best for His kingdom. To this day, we will find ourselves thinking of each other and feel a need to get together. Occasionally, it is because I need a session or so about a certain topic. But those times are few a far between now. Now it's more about having breakfast together and catching up with our separate lives.

Once I had my life put together in Christ, I found out that my role for the rest of my life would be to fight

Satan. It is now my job to bring hurting women to God and His kingdom. Many times, it is after wrestling them away from Satan's control. It is my job to help other women find the freedom in Christ that I have and to help them identify what God has for them to do for His kingdom.

The enemy had so affected control over my family for generations. It would take God's blessings and work from me, with the help of my mentors, to break off those generational curses and replace them with His generational blessings. Since God always wins over Lucifer, with His help, so do I. I want this for all my ladies as well.

My family, from me on down, is no longer under the generational curses that a satanic cult places within generations of families for as long as we allow them to remain. My extended time of wrestling with Lucifer and winning has put me in a place of taking control of him. Because of my relationship with my heavenly Father, I will always in one way or another be battling Lucifer. I realize that that experience of conquering Lucifer and replacing his control of my life with my Creator's puts me in a place to fight with Satan for others and win freedom for them.

As you may already know, the deliverance process is not an easy process but certainly available when the time is right. There are various Christian members trained to help others become delivered from the hold Satan has on them. It is well worth it in the end.

There is a whole procedure for taking your life back from Lucifer and giving it to God that can be done when needed. It is not something to be tried if you have not had the training. It is the closest you will come to direct, hand-to-hand combat with the enemy. And Satan is fighting his hardest to keep you in captivity.

The enemy gets particularly mad at you when you are fighting to bring God to others. Once you achieve your own deliverance, you are able, with training, to help others achieve their freedom too. See Isaiah 61:1:

The spirit of the Sovereign Lord is on me, because the Lord has anointed me to proclaim good news to the poor. He has sent me to bind up the brokenhearted, to proclaim freedom for the captives and release from darkness for the prisoners.

From my own counseling experiences, I know that there are many hurting women out there who don't want anything to do with God. Some believe He exists, but in their minds, He has failed them. Others are not sure that there really is a God.

I've heard it often, "If there is a God, why am I being abused? Don't talk to me about God! He isn't available to me. Where was He when I needed Him?"

Through my testimony, I become a real victim to victor to them, not just a counselor. I tell them about my past experiences of sexual abuse as a child. By becoming transparent, I share examples of the poor decisions I made in my life as an adult because of my hurting childhood. Most women can identify with me.

Because of my success in finding freedom and joy that they can see in me for themselves, women usually, given time, trust me with information they have never shared with anyone else. Here is someone they can risk being honest with and not be judged by. The fear that they will shock me or tell me something so unacceptable to me is no longer a risk to them.

God has allowed me to feel freedom from the shame of my past. The women see that. These hurting women are eventually more open to working with God even though they still may not trust Him, because they now trust me. They crave the freedom from their past too.

What an opportunity God has placed in my life. It's a responsibility that I am honored to carry with His presence constantly as my guide. It's only through my Lord that any of this works as well as it does. I love bringing more and more ladies to His kingdom and love hearing how their growth in Him is affecting others. Many ladies want to give back what God gave to them and find a way to do that for His kingdom. They gain freedom and confidence. This helps them to do what they might not have chosen to do without those sessions with their Lord.

What a difference it is to remember the lady who walked through my back door at the beginning of our time together compared to the present lady standing before me at the end of all her sessions. The Lord has triumphed again! I make sure they see the difference as part of our last time together.

What a three-stranded cord we have become!

> Though one may be overpowered, two can defend themselves. A cord of three strands is not quickly broken. (Ecclesiastes 4:12)

So, who am I really, now that I have found me? I am someone *in God's service, which makes me whole, happy, and fulfilled.* (Who can ask for more than this?)

Do I still have bad days along with the good? Absolutely. Does life go on in a continual state of calm, peace, and perfection? No way. I still have neuropathy and have trouble walking. I still have days where everything I try goes wrong, but I handle it all differently.

Each day I talk to God as if He is standing right beside me, as my best friend, sometimes out loud, sometimes to myself. "Lord, thank You for this great parking place! God, things aren't going well today. If these things are not from You, Lord, I need to know. (So, Satan get out of my life in the name of Jesus.) Holy Spirit, nudge me when it's my turn to 'talk God' today. Jesus, help that poor woman with her pain."

Some days I fail at what I have spent time over the years teaching to my ladies. I get in a hard place or lose my peace over something. My emotions get in the way of my logic. God will say to me, "What would you tell your ladies in the same situation?" Humbling? Absolutely!

It helps me to remember how much I need my Lord to guide me each moment for as long as I remain here on His earth.

Dear heavenly Deliverer,

> How can I ever live up to the authority and anointing you have placed in my life? Without you it would be impossible (Philippians 4:13).

> I understand that it is a gift given to me because of the preparation You have completed within me. Because of what the enemy had meant for harm to me and my family, I have been chosen to take others from that same captive life and bring them to You. Only through You, Jesus, who died for our sins and left behind the Holy Spirit who dwells in

us constantly, will I be able to show Your honor and glory.

Thank You, heavenly Father, for Your sacrifice of Your Son and His resurrection to show us that we too can be resurrected. Jesus, it is only through all your sacrifice that I and others have been able to come from our sin-filled past to fulfill the true reason you placed us here on earth.

Dear, mighty God of Jacob, help me to constantly defeat the enemy for myself, my family, and others. I pray that I continue to open my eyes, ears, and spirit to Your ever-present guidance. Help me to lead others to the joy, freedom, and peace You have always meant for us to have in abundance. I pray these things in Your name, amen.

The thief comes only to steal and kill and destroy; I have come that they may have life, and have it to the full. (John 10:10)

BOOK II

1

Women of the Bible: Yesterday and Today

Let's look first to see what God, through scripture, has to say about who we are as women in Christ and how important He thinks we are to His kingdom.

You decide which one of these women is the current version of you. At least one of them will remind you of yourself. Are there some things written here that you did not know about any of the women listed?

Since God started life on earth with Eve as the first women, we too will start our list of women of the Bible with Eve. We are not talking *The Three Faces of Eve*, Eve. We are talking about Adam's Eve, the Eve created from a rib from the side of man, both of whom were created by God, not created by fiction to increase the ratings.

Eve: Adam's Wife, She Shall Be Called Woman

Adam was working away at his assignment from God, and God decided Adam needed a help-mate (Genesis 2:18, 21–25). So out of the side of an unconscious Adam comes a rib that becomes Eve.

Think about this—Eve, like Adam, was never born as we are all born into this world. Not only did she not have a mother or earthly father, but she also was born into a world without sin. Therefore, she was not able to sin until the forbidden fruit deal.

I wonder how she and Adam decided who does the cooking and who takes out the garbage. Were they the originators of rock, paper, scissors?

In the honeymoon phase of their marriage, they worked well together. But as in all marriages, along comes life. Eve, with Adam's and Satan's help, delivered the first sin before she delivered her first child (Genesis 3:1–13). Satan, in the form of a snake, put temptation in front of a human for the first time. Because of this failure to follow God's instructions, God, like all good parents, handed out the penalty with loving disapproval.

We, ladies, have Eve to thank for our labor pains (Genesis 3:16). Beside the labor pains for Eve, Adam and Eve were given rules on what is considered appropriate attire (Genesis 3:21). Not only were they told what to wear, but they were also told where they are no longer allowed to hang out.

Sound like your house with your kids? You have told your kids they are no longer allowed to go to the mall. And those outfits! "You will not leave the house looking like that again."

God kicked them out of the garden of Eden (Genesis

3:20–24). And those garments of animal skin now had
to be worn always. No more of this naked stuff for you.
Just as in the modern day, parents and children have
been battling clothes and where they are forbidden to
go now that they messed up.

Moving into the next phase of Adam and Eve's
marriage, along come two children back to back
(Genesis 4:1–2) and then a third child (Genesis 4:25).
Eve was suffering labor pains as well as the fact that
she had a bad kid. Her sons were quarreling, and her
oldest killed his younger brother (Genesis 4:8). Her
great-great-great-great-grandkids were not doing so
well either (Genesis 4:23).

After all that, she was not given equal billing of
importance in her role on earth. She was not listed, as
the men of the Bible are, as far as how long she lived.
The first woman is not given honor equal to the first
man's honor. Adam's years on earth are listed at 930
years (Genesis 5:5), but nowhere that I could find were
Eve's years on earth listed.

So Moses, who is credited with writing Genesis
(listed in the foreword for the book of Genesis in my
NIV Bible) was already putting a wedge between equality of the sexes. Not God but a human started that
process. Well, Moses, we forgive you. You had other
fine qualities.

Eve was the first lady of the world and the first
mother, but mothers in general, at least in biblical
times, must not have had the advantage of a book of
baby names to help them name their children. Many
women who followed Eve carried the same name,
Mary. There are at least six Mary's we need to separate out in our minds. Of this group, Mary, mother of

Jesus, leads the way. Speaking of mothers, there is no comparison!

Mary: Mother of Jesus Christ, "Let It Be to Me According to Your Word" (NKJV)

No other title is required to distinguish her from the rest. The angel Gabriel appeared to a very young Mary to announce her future (Luke 1:26–38).

Surprise, Mary! Talk about one second your life is going as you have planned it and the next second your life is completely turned around. How do you wrap your head around something like this? They're never going to believe this back at the office.

Mary did not get to pick the name of her own child, among other restrictions in her life (Isaiah 7:14). And I do wonder if what happens to many of us happened to her. So often we say yes to something with our own preconceived ideas of what that will entail. Then when we are in the thick of what we said yes to, we say something like, "I didn't think this would be like this." Or "I had no idea what I was getting into."

After Gabriel explained to Mary that she was the chosen one, she accepted what was told to her as the truth and was determined to fill her role (Luke 1:38). As happens in more modern times, Mary knew that since she was unmarried and pregnant, she would be rejected in her neighborhood and family, so, she went to spend time with her cousin Elizabeth, who was carrying John the Baptist in her womb (Luke 1:39–45, 56).

Mary was very surprised, yet again, when Elizabeth greeted her as the mother of the Lord. Not only did Elizabeth greet Mary in a surprised fashion, but Elizabeth's baby also leaped for joy in her womb

(Luke 1:44). Feeling she was in a better place for right now, Mary stayed there for three months. Mary must have wondered how Elizabeth knew she was carrying Jesus. This was well before cell phones!

Could you imagine being Mary? First the unexpected pregnancy and now Elizabeth's reaction to her as the mother of the Lord, and on top of that, Elizabeth's baby reacts to Mary's presence. "How did Elizabeth know? Who else knows? What am I going to do next? I can't stay here forever."

I am sure she thought she would be a single parent. Joseph would never marry her now. Where would she live? How would she be able to raise this child alone? Who was going to believe her story?

But as we all know, God worked out all the details, and Joseph did become her husband (Matthew 1:20–25). Of all times to have to travel, Joseph and Mary needed to travel to Bethlehem on business around the time of Mary's due date. And as any good writer would have written into her script, Mary went into labor and delivered our Savior in a manger (Luke 2:5–19).

Even without Twitter, lots of others found out about the birth and came to see the baby. On the eighth day, the law of Moses required a circumcision (Luke 2:21–39). Mary was told more about who this Son she had delivered in a manger would become.

Like all teenagers, Jesus was trying His best to be an adult a little too soon, which put Mary and Joseph in an uncomfortable place. They were unable to find Him while they were traveling (Luke 2:41–51). Not only did Jesus step out before His time, but there also were times when even Mary got it wrong as to what Jesus was supposed to do while here on earth (John 2:1–10).

This time it was Jesus who became uncomfortable

about what Mary was asking Him to do. Mary thought changing water into wine would be a nice gesture for the crowd of friends at the wedding. Eventually, they both got it right, and Jesus went throughout the area talking about His heavenly Father and healing the sick.

This is all well and good, but at one point His family became concerned about Him and decided to have a chat about what He was doing and saying (Matthew 12:46–50). I can't imagine how Mary and His brothers must have felt when Jesus rejected them. He rejected them by not coming out of a home to speak to her and His family. After all she had been through, the least He could do is take a minute to talk to her. But they must have made things right between them at some point because later Mary was there for her Son when He was crucified (John 19:25–27, Mark 15:40).

I am totally unable to fathom myself doing what Mary did. How much pain was in her heart as she watched her Son hang on the cross! I would have totally lost it in some way. Her heavenly Father had to help her with that. It is the only answer!

Jesus assigned John to care for Mary as if they were mother and son. Joseph seemed to be nowhere in the picture by this time. Since Mary and Joseph had other children whom one would guess would care for their mom after Jesus's death, I can't help but wonder why John was given that assignment. Don't get me wrong—it was quite nice that Jesus did that for her. I'm just not sure exactly why a blood-related brother was not given the assignment. I can make guesses, but no facts that I could find addressed my question.

Mary recovered from Jesus's death enough to become involved in the mechanics or politics of the disciple group (Acts 1:12–14). She helped pray for a replacement for the man who helped to have her son killed. Judas Iscariot took himself out of the mix when he killed himself (Matthew 27:5). Someone needed to take his place.

And how hard was it for Mary to forgive Judas? While she knew in her spirit what Jesus was brought into this world to do, it still must have been hard to forgive anyone who took your son from you.

Also, how hard was it not to try to avoid or prevent Jesus's death? He was still her baby. He was still her son. Would I change my mind the closer it got to His death?

After Jesus's death, I am sure there were other ways she became involved in strengthening and supporting the reason God put Jesus on earth. What an unbelievably strong woman she was! What a role model she continues to be for other women! In hard times, tell yourself, "If Mary lived through watching her son be crucified, I should be able to handle this."

Mary Magdalene: Had Seven Demons Removed by Jesus, "Go Tell His Disciples and Peter"

This is another Mary who can easily stand on her own in the Bible. Her most important role was declaring Jesus's resurrection to the disciples (Mark 16:9–10, John 20:1–2, John 20:11–18).

Jesus picked a woman who was just as much a disciple, in Jesus's mind, as any of the men to announce His resurrection (John 20)! Mary Magdalene went to the tomb to find the stone had already been moved away. Jesus was no longer there. She ran to the rest of the disciples to tell them Jesus was gone. They would not believe her story. They all went to the tomb to find out that Mary Magdalene did know what she was talking about but left again not understanding what was happening.

Mary Magdalene stayed behind at the tomb after all the others left. As she cried standing at the tomb, she saw two angels in white (John 20:10–18). They asked why she was crying. During her response, she turned and saw Jesus standing there. She did not recognize Him at first. But in a short time, she figured out who He was. Jesus gave her specific instructions as to how to deal with His death and how to deal with the other disciples. She returned to the disciples, explaining what happened to her after they left the tomb.

What if someone had told Mary Magdalene she could not tell the disciples that Jesus had risen because she was a woman? And worse—what if she *didn't do* what Jesus was asking her to do because of what *someone else* told her she could not do? Don't stop affecting the kingdom of God because *someone else* told you that you can't do something because you are a woman. If God has given you that assignment, He is the only one who needs to sign off on it.

Her past may not have been the purest of the group (Mark 16:9), yet Mary Magdalene was still present at His crucifixion (Mark 15:40, Matthew 27:56). All the responsibility was given to her by Jesus to announce His resurrection, even though her introduction to Jesus was not the best. He cast seven demons out of her. However, she then became one of the women who traveled with and supported the disciples (Luke 8:1–3). What if, as a rabbi, Jesus would have judged her only by her past?

Many insist she was a prostitute, but nowhere in the Bible, that I was able to find, was that actually stated as her means of support before she met Jesus. How she got those demons was never mentioned.

Research online has her listed from prostitute to saint depending upon the article. Maybe she was just like the rest of us. Maybe she made some bad decisions at one time in her life. Once she realized her mistakes, repentance and freedom from her sins made her a different woman.

It would be great if we all would get life right at the first shot. Some of us do. But many of us don't do so well at first. But as Mary Magdalene discovered, we all have a chance to turn our lives around. Many times, God uses what we learned during our difficult years. He turns what were our weaknesses into strengths so we can help others to learn about God's mercy and grace. My years of sexual abuse and poor decision-making because of that abuse were not a waste. I needed those experiences so I could identify with and help others.

Mary: Sister of Martha, Also Known as Mary of Bethany

Mary also had a brother named Lazarus who added to this Mary's reputation. Even those who have never read the Bible know about Lazarus being raised from the dead (John 11:1–14). This alone put Martha and Mary on everyone's radar.

Before the resurrection happened, Jesus stopped at their house on His travels (Luke 10:38–42). He would visit various times as a place of rest. Mary sat at His feet listening while Martha was trying to prepare the meal. Martha, in her frustration, told Jesus she wanted Mary to help her, but Jesus felt otherwise (Luke 10:41–42).

Often when we woman talk about each other, you will hear, "She is such a Martha." As much as Martha was known for her obsession with the mechanics of that day, so Mary is also known for the worship she showed to Jesus that day.

Mary, Martha, and Lazarus were loved by Jesus (John 11:5). Mary seemed to do more crying than Martha and had a harder time pulling it together. But Mary's ways spoke volumes as far as being used as an evangelist. Those trying to comfort her in the house after Lazarus's death followed her to the grave site as she left the house to see Jesus. Therefore, she was responsible for bringing a large part of the audience Jesus wanted to be present for the resurrection of Lazarus. Mary, along with the rest, could witness Jesus raising her brother from the dead (John 11:1–44).

In John 11:2 in my NIV Bible in parentheses, it states that this Mary, whose brother Lazarus lay sick, was the Mary who poured oil on Jesus's feet and wiped his feet with her hair. This was done in Bethany at Simon the Leper's house (John11:2, John 12:3 NIV).[7]

---

[7] Of all the research I did for this book, trying to figure out the Mary's and who poured oil on the feet or the head of Jesus took the longest to research and had the least-satisfying results. I won't go into the debates and why it is felt that the one was Mary Magdalene and yet in another area of research it is thought to be Mary, sister of Martha. You take a whack at the research.

I also found a listing on the internet that feels Mary Magdalene did neither of these. One of the Mary's thought to be a participant was listed as a sinner. And while we all sin, Mary Magdalene took sinning to a different height than Mary, Martha's sister.

As best I can figure out, anointing the feet was Mary, Martha's sister, as I stated above. So, I listed the head anointing below. The more I looked, the more confused I got. And I am sure

There are a few other Mary's to talk about.

One is Mary, the sister of Mary, Jesus's mother, who was also the mother of James and Joseph (John 19: 25, Luke 24:10, Matthew 27:56). The sister was often referred to as the other Mary (Matthew 27:61, Matthew 28:1).

Another Mary is the one who labored with Paul (Romans 16:6).

The last Mary we will look at was the mother of John Mark also called Mark (Acts 12:12).

Hopefully that has helped you figure out Mary who? Or maybe now you are more confused if you have never paused long enough to think that through. Let's leave the Mary's and go to the following two interesting women associated with a Mary listed above.

Anna: An Eight-Four-Year-Old Jewish Prophetess Who Prayed over an Eight-Day-Old Jesus

Anna met Jesus when He was taken to the temple to be circumcised. Did you ever wonder why it happened on day eight?

There are various religious reasons supported by various religious groups. However, once a nurse, always a nurse. Medically, God knew what He was doing long before humankind did. A clotting factor is at its all-time high eight days after birth. Back then, they

---

those of you who are students of the Bible to a depth that few of us attain may have other ideas. Add to this confusion of the Mary's, some articles stated that Simon the Leper may not be the same as Simon the Pharisee. I had to lay down and take a nap after all this!

A Mary is credited with being the Mary that poured perfume on the head (instead of the feet) of Jesus before His death (Matthew 26:7, Mark 14:3–9).

also did not have any medication they could use to enhance the clotting factor as we do today.

In today's world of circumcision, any day is a good day medically with the addition of clotting medicines. However, in Jesus's day, Dr. God made sure the circumcisions were done on the optimal day. (I am sure I have lost some men at this point. At very least I am sure you have tightly crossed your legs and tightened up your lap. Sorry ...)

Anna was widowed after only seven years with her husband. She never left the temple but stayed and prayed and fasted. Anna foretold who Jesus was to become (Luke 2:36–38). What a role she had in the day of women having few religious responsibilities! Woman were not to be believed or at very least didn't know enough to count. She was put in place by God for a specific purpose, which she fulfilled.

There are those of you who feel you can't find the reason God put you here on earth and worry that you don't have a direction yet. Here is your woman of the Bible. You have been seeking and asking and feeling left out. Your other friends have heard from God and are living their purpose. But you feel you haven't a clue as to your assignment.

> Here is your role model. Here is where
> you find peace!

You may be in place for a moment of time to come. And you may be eighty-four years old when it happens. Don't give up your relationship with God because you feel He is not communicating your purpose to you. There will be things along the way that you will do without realizing that you affected His kingdom that day as you were supposed to do.

It can be as simple as a smile you extended to a cashier at the grocery store who is having the worst day of her life. Your smile brought her a moment of peace and a good feeling that she needed right at that time.

Keep honoring God, and He will honor you by putting you in others' lives as His representative at just the right time and place. The cashier may not have recognized it, but she saw the spirit of Jesus in your smile. She felt His peace for just a second in her hard time that day.

Relax in the knowledge that your purpose will show up when it is supposed to show up. I am sure that Anna had other God moments besides the one she is most famous for listed above. God would not have wasted the energy Anna used in her fasting and prayers. He had to have used her for other situations. Those other ways just did not make it into the Bible.

Your efforts will not be wasted either! Whatever you are doing now or while waiting on your purpose to show will be preparing you for your future. It may not feel like that to you. It certainly didn't feel that way to David either.

David had been anointed by Samuel to become king someday but found himself back out in the fields. First, he had to take care of Goliath (1Samuel 17). What did this have to do with becoming king? Then he had to deal with Saul's hate for him (1 Samuel 19). David must have been thinking, *Samuel has lost his mind. There is no way I will ever become king.* But we all know the ending to this! He became a great king.

Be alert to your everyday happenings. React to

them as God's ambassador would react. That ambassador is you!

Martha: Sister of Mary and Lazarus

Her name is used today to describe women more interested in checking things off their to-do lists than taking time for what's truly important in the moment. "Praying with that woman that just lost her husband in this accident is not on my to-do list for today, so I'll just keep walking past. I'll be late if I stop. Someone else will take care of it."

"You are such a Martha!" I have heard this more than once in my lifetime. Hopefully it was not as bad as the sentence above, and hopefully I continue to make improvements in this area. But there are times I must keep practicing spontaneity to keep improving on my Martha ways.

When Jesus came to Lazarus, Mary, and Martha's house to preach, Martha was more interested in getting her tasks done than listening to Jesus (Luke 10:38–42). Yet by the time it came for Jesus to raise her brother Lazarus from the dead, Martha was 100 percent sure of what Jesus could do and who He was (John 11:1–44).

Bill Crowder in one of his *Daily Bread Insight* statements confirms,

> Martha, Lazarus's sister, is one of the most misunderstood characters in the New Testament. We usually think of her in the context of Luke 10:38–42, where Jesus challenges her misdirected priorities. This often leads to the conclusion that she was somehow spiritually inferior

to her sister, Mary. However, Martha is the one who expresses her confidence in Christ to do something about the death of her brother (John 11:21–22). And she makes a wonderful statement on the deity of Christ, showing that she, in fact, had great depth of spiritual understanding (v. 27).

I am wondering if she did what many of we multitaskers do, meaning we learn how to work and listen at the same time, therefore doing neither task very well. Or maybe she finally learned to forget her to-do list.

In "All the Women of the Bible" on Biblegateway. com, Martha is listed as the oldest of the three. Those of us who are the oldest in our families know that we tend to be the leaders, the one out front. Since she was the oldest, it was her house. When Jesus finally came back to raise Lazarus from the dead, Martha was the one who went out to meet Him (John 11:20). Mary stayed behind and did not come out until Martha went back to tell her that Jesus wanted to see her.

Like Martha, how many of us have started out our day with our own schedule and timing planned, only to have to lay that schedule down? It becomes plain to us as the day progresses that God has other plans for this day, none of which is on our to-do list. Lord, You gave us this day to begin with. It should be Yours to plan!

Let's look at another mother of interest, one associated with Mary, mother of Jesus. Elizabeth is already mentioned above in the write-up about Mary.

Elizabeth: Mother to John the Baptist and Cousin to Mary, Mother of Jesus

Elizabeth, along with her husband Zacharias, were up in years and had no children. She was related to Mary, the mother of Jesus, a cousin (Luke 1:36). An angel, Gabriel, appeared to Zacharias to break the news to him that Elizabeth was going to have a child. Gabriel told them not only that it would be a boy but that they also should name him John (Luke 1:13–17). John was not a family name, which was how most children were named at that time.

They also found out from Gabriel that John would do great things, and therefore here is what you are to feed him and not feed him. Gabriel provided Elizabeth and Zacharias with other suggestions as to how to raise their child. Elizabeth and Zacharias had just experienced the first child-birthing class!

Another aspect of Elizabeth's role as mother to John is that John, who would pave the way for the Lord, was a pure-blooded priest. Both Elizabeth and Zacharias were from a priestly line of Aaron (Luke 1:5). So, paving the way of Christ was a man who had lived in the wilderness all his life until called out to prepare others. I must wonder if he was sent to the wilderness as a protection from society. I am guessing it is harder to sin when you are alone in the woods and away from worldly temptation.

In Elizabeth's sixth month, Mary appeared at her house for refuge. Yet, without Facebook to announce to Mary's friends and relatives what just happened to her, Elizabeth greeted Mary as the mother of the Lord (Luke 1:43). And immediately, John, her baby, leaped for joy in Elizabeth's womb (Luke 1:44). Mary had to be taken aback by Elizabeth's greeting.

While I am sure Elizabeth was in awe about having Mary, the mother of the Lord, in her house and about her son John, who was to become important, I must wonder about a few things. Things like how Elizabeth felt about some angel that she didn't see, only her husband saw, giving her specific instructions on the name of her baby and how to raise him. As a protective first-time mother who had waited years to become a mother, would she feel she could take care of her child as she saw fit (thank you very much)? Or as a new first-time mother, unsure of her role, since she hadn't been responsible for a child before, was it a relief to have some direction?

If you add in the fact that after doubting the angel, her husband couldn't speak, what must Elizabeth have been thinking about this angel (Luke 1:20)? One of her thoughts might have been, *So if I don't follow what the angel tells me to do, what will he do to me? Look what he did to my husband.*

Whatever her thoughts, she and Zacharias turned out a great man. John the Baptist went out into the world to work for God's kingdom by preparing the way for Jesus (Matthew 3, Mark 1). If it were up to the family, John would have had a family name instead of John as told by Gabriel. The strong, mature woman, Elizabeth, spoke up and insisted on the name of John (Luke 1:60). While Zacharias was punished by Gabriel because of his unbelief, Elizabeth seemed to have no doubt in God's messenger.

Not all mothers were as good at their job as Elizabeth. There are several examples of the types of bad mothers, but one of the first conniving mothers is Rebekah.

Rebekah: Wife of Isaac, Mother of Jacob and Esau

Abraham's son Isaac needed a bride (Genesis 24). Abraham sent his servant with specific instructions to find a wife for his son. The most specific instruction was that God's angel would be involved in the match-making. The servant included prayer in his desire to make the right choice. Before the servant finished praying, God delivered.

Rebekah, a beautiful virgin, came to fill her water jar where Abraham's servant was praying. She was good to the servant and his animals, and the servant felt that God had blessed him with the right wife for Isaac. Rebekah took the servant back to her home. With a few gifts, here and a little negotiation there, the deal was sealed. Rebekah agreed to go, looking forward to meeting her husband to be.

Rebekah was brought back to Isaac, and they were married. While not all planned marriages work out well, this one did. Isaac loved her (Genesis 24:67). Despite the twenty-year age difference, their marriage was good. The marriage remained childless for twenty years. But Isaac prayed, and she became pregnant with twins (Genesis 25:21–26).

Esau and Jacob, like many siblings, were competitive. Rebekah's favorite child was Jacob. When Isaac was very old, and partially blind, he knew it was time to bless his oldest, Esau, before he died. Isaac gave Esau an assignment to do before the blessing could be given.

Rebekah heard all this (Genesis 27:5–45). She wanted her favorite, Jacob, to get the blessing instead of Esau. So she came up with an in-depth plan to make that happen. She thought of everything, which worked well for what she wanted it to do. Jacob got the blessing, but it was not Rebekah's most shining moment in the eyes of God.

Again, there were varying articles about this online. Most agreed the lovely and loving Rebekah during the first twenty years of their marriage changed to a completely different woman after she had her children. Some of the articles support Rebekah in the decisions she made since Jacob was to be the blessed leader, not Esau. They feel she was supporting the Lord's choice. Other articles felt what she did was not appropriate and not done because of God's prophecy. What Rebekah did caused the demise of a family that some authors felt should not have happened.

We can all relate to things we wish we would have handled differently in our past. I wonder if Rebekah felt any remorse later in life, or was she pleased with what she did even up to her deathbed? Did the twins wish that they could have been closer than they were? God had informed Rebekah at the time of her pregnancy that the twins would be separated in life (Genesis 25:23). So was she reacting to God's plan or her own?

How would you handle a situation if you were not in agreement with it? We all want to please our Lord, but I know I would have had difficulty allowing my sons to separate to that extent. They were fighting for the rest of their lives.

My sons are thirteen months apart and were extremely close growing up. Now, family responsibilities, work requirements, and life in general do not allow much time for them to continue to be as close as they were.

But when they do come together, I still see that closeness in the way they respond to each other. If

God would have told me that they would be even more distanced than they are, I would have had a hard time supporting that prophecy. It looks like Rebekah reacted in a way that encouraged the separation. However, I was not walking in Rebekah's shoes thankfully.

Hopefully some of you are seeing yourselves in one of these women, or maybe other women to come on the following pages. Be encouraged to know that you too, at whatever age you are, doing whatever you are doing now or not doing, can be influential to God's work. If the Bible were being written today, you could be mentioned in it. I am sure many, if not all, of these ladies had no idea they would show up on God's radar for publication in His book.

Many of the women we are learning about became famous because of who they begot. These two ladies, with the help of their female servants, together begot enough children to provide a leader for each of the twelve tribes of Israel. Here are examples of being famous because of their children.

Leah: Jacob's First Wife, Sister to Rachel, Mother to Leaders of Nations

While Leah was Jacob's first wife, she was not his favorite for a long time. He was in love with a prettier, younger Rachel and expected to marry Rachel on his wedding day. He had worked seven long years to claim her. Jacob's father-in-law-to-be played a trick on Jacob and switched sisters for Leah to be Jacob's first bride without Jacob realizing it (Genesis 29:15–30).

Talk about what goes around comes around. Jacob, under his mother's tutelage, cheated Esau out of his heritage (although Esau had already given away his firstborn status to Jacob for some soup, Genesis

25:29–32), just as Laban cheated Jacob out of Rachel for Leah. It was tradition then that the oldest must marry first before the second and so on. Laban dressed Leah up so that Jacob could not tell the difference until after they had consummated the marriage.

How would you feel being replaced after only one week of marriage? While Jacob had to work an additional seven years for Rachel, his heart remained with Rachel, not Leah. She stayed married to a man whom she knew loved not only another woman but her younger sister. What does that do to a sister relationship? So, no loving husband and having to watch your younger sister as the wife Jacob adored more than you. What a hurtful life Leah must have had.

Even when God provided Leah with lots of sons, and Rachel with no children for a time (Genesis 30:1–2), Leah still felt unloved and felt herself a second-class citizen in Jacob's eyes (Genesis 29:31–35).

With the birth of each of her first four children, Leah was sure that Jacob would surely love her now. Having sons would normally in that time elevate the woman in society. And maybe it did help Leah within her society, but her true wish was for the affection of her husband. After four sons, she stopped having children for a while (Genesis 29:35).

Since there was no birth control in those days, I must wonder if Leah cut off having relations with Jacob at this point. She may have felt, *Why bother? I give you sons, you give me nothing.* So maybe during this time, Jacob had to sleep on the couch when he visited Leah's house!

While her sons all led a tribe of Israel, one of those sons, Judah, was the biggest feather in Leah's hat. At that time Leah would have no way of knowing that

Judah would be part of Jesus's lineage. Of the twelve tribes, our Messiah came as the Lion of the Tribe of Judah (Matthew 1:1–17). Zilpah, Leah's maid, gave Jacob two sons also (Genesis 30:9–13).

One of the most interesting things I learned in my research is that, in the end, it was Leah whom Jacob honored by burying her in the family grave plot that included Abraham, Sarah, Isaac, and Rebekah (Genesis 49:31).

Rachel, as you will remember, died and was buried on the way to Ephrath, where Jacob erected a monument in her honor. But Leah died later and was buried in the family cave. While Leah felt unloved by worldly standards, the love she received from her Lord provided justice for her through the inheritance of her lineage that blessed the world with Jesus Christ our Savior.

Rachel: Second Wife of Jacob's, Mother to Joseph and Benjamin

Rachel was Jacob's favorite wife even though he had to work an additional seven years for her father. To marry Rachel after his first unplanned marriage to Leah, Jacob promised an additional seven years of work for her father (Genesis 29:9–12, 16–31). And even though God gave Leah sons and Rachel none at first, Rachel remained the more loved, more beautiful, younger wife in Jacob's eyes (Genesis 30:1–8, 22–34).

Maybe it was because of the pain of having to wait so long for her two children to come, or that she was so angry with her father for what he had done by switching her out with her sister, that at one point Rachel changed from a good girl of the Bible to a bad girl of the Bible (Genesis 31:19, 33–35).

When her father was away, Rachel stole items from his home. And when her father caught up to the fleeing family of Jacob, Rachel sat on the stolen items and hid them from her father. She used her monthly period as an excuse for not getting up when her father entered the tent looking for the items.

We will never know what changed Rachel. But up until this time, there is no mention of her as a schemer or a thief. As the one Jacob loved the most, one would think that her life was easier than Leah's life.

Maybe not having children or Leah having children or who knows what pressures Rachel may have lived with caused the change in her behavior. Having expectations and not being able to achieve them can leave us hurt, depressed, and ashamed, even if those expectations were unreal expectations to begin with.

Jacob's love for Rachel was not able to keep her from death in childbirth with her second child, Benjamin. Jacob still had his family on the road when Rachel died. There was a burial outside the family tomb (Genesis 35:16–20, 48:7). Bilhah was Rachel's maid, who gave Jacob another two of his sons (Genesis 30:3–8).

A quick note here for Bilhah and Zilpah the maids. It appears that if you are a maid to someone, more often than not, you wind up being a concubine to the husband of the woman who is your mistress. So, if you were the maid, it would be just as important to you who your mistress would marry. Wonder if any maids back in that time helped to influence their mistress on her choice. If I knew my status and the turn of events that were to follow, would I finagle who I would wind up with as much as I could? Would I just accept that decision to fate?

God loved Rachel and Bilhah just as much as He loved Leah and Zilpah and just as much as He loves you right now just as you are. We humans differentiate our love for each other, but God does not. When we disappoint Him, He never disowns us. Even when we have times like Rachel and Rebekah of not acting like the great Christian woman God would like us to be, He forgives and does not disown.

Thank You, God, for Your mercy and grace." In return, something that's hard for us to do is give God back that mercy and grace when we feel He is not doing in our lives what we think He should be doing. When He disappoints us, many of us don't forgive and *do disown*. We walk away from Him. He never walks away from us.

Here is another example of using your servant to get what God had promised. When we don't see it happening as promised, we do things something like what Sarah did thinking we are helping God to fulfill His promise to us. We are not being helpful at all!

Sarah: Wife of Abraham, Half-Sister of Abraham, and Isaac's mother.

Abraham and Sarah had the same father but a different mother. At that time, it was permissible to marry if there were different mothers. Sarah was considered the mother of nations.

Her beauty was well documented since twice Abraham asked her to tell others she was his sister (Genesis 12:10–20, 20:1–18). As Abraham's half-sister, that was not entirely a lie. She was also his wife. Sarah is also noted because she called Abraham lord.

Like many other women, Sarah was unable to have children as quickly as she wanted to. Even though

Abraham was promised by God that His offspring would number the stars in the sky, it wasn't happening with them (Genesis 15:1–5). Sarah gave her maid, Hagar, to Abraham to start the family (Genesis 16:1–4). After Hagar became pregnant, she and Sarah did not get along.

Hagar ran away. An angel came to Hagar and told her about her son that she was carrying, Ismael, and who he was to become (Genesis 16:8–12). Hagar returned to Abraham and Sarah before Ismael's birth.

At another time, Abraham welcomed strangers to his tent and asked Sarah to prepare a meal for them (Genesis 18:6–15). During that meal, one of them prophesied about a son for Sarah and Abraham. She was listening and laughed because both she and Abraham were well past the time of having children. But a year later, as promised, along came Isaac, whose name means laughter (Genesis 21:1–7).

In today's world, does that mean if I giggle during the conception of my child, I need to name them Giggle? Hmmm, I think not!

After all that waiting to have that promised child, I can't imagine what Sarah might have thought of God's testing of Abraham to include the possible death of her son, Isaac (Genesis 22:1–19). The Bible doesn't mention how or when or even if Sarah knew about the incident.

Even if she didn't know about it at the time it was happening, what a shock to find out that her husband was ready to sacrifice her son as Abraham had been ready to do. If that angel would not have come and stopped Abraham from killing Isaac, we would be reading a different story (Genesis 22:1–19).

How would I feel about my husband after he returned with a story such as Abraham and Isaac must

have had in the end? Would I beat my husband over
the head with his own staff and say, "What were you
thinking?" Or would I say nothing and be thankful
that he was obedient to God and God responded as
He did?

But Sarah received something that most women of
the Bible did not receive, and that was that she was
honored as the men were honored in the Bible. Sarah
lived 127 years, and it was recorded and included in
the Bible.

Even though she was nine years younger than
Abraham, she died first (Genesis 23:1–20). Another
first celebrated by Sarah was that Abraham went
against the tradition of burying your dead while on
the road. He invested in a vault in which not only were
he and Sarah buried but so were Isaac and Rebekah
and Jacob and Leah.

On to some other mothers who were honored because of who they begot or what they did for their
husband.

Hagar: Egyptian Handmaiden of Sarah, Mother of Ismael

Much of what you need to know about Hagar, you have
read above. But let's look a little closer at the information. When Sarah was unable to conceive, she decided
to help God out with His prophecy about having a
child. As was done in that time, Sarah gave Hagar to
Abraham (Genesis 16:1–16). She bore a son, Ishmael.
However, there was a lot of drama between conception
and birth.

When Hagar learned she was pregnant, she developed contempt for Sarah. Sarah took the issue to
Abraham, and he told her to handle it herself (Genesis

16:3–6). As Sarah continued to treat Hagar harshly, Hagar fled.

It states in the Bible that an angel of the Lord found Hagar and spoke with her (Genesis 16:7–16). Hagar was told to return to her mistress. She was also told all about the son she would be having. Hagar was told about his personality and that he would be cared for by God. So Hagar returned to Sarah and had Ismael, Abraham's son.

While Hagar was feeling like a second-class citizen and that she was being treated unfairly, she did not realize that this was the first time in the Bible where God revealed Himself. She was the first person since Adam and Eve to have God appear and make a significant difference in someone's life. Since the Bible, of course, was not written yet, how would she know?

As Ishmael continued to grow and was older than Isaac, the child Sarah and Abraham had together, Sarah became unhappy with the boys growing up together. She told Abraham that the slave woman and her son must go (Genesis 21:9–21). This time Abraham was the one telling Hagar she must leave. He gave them water and bread and sent them on their way. In the wilderness, it was not long until Hagar ran out of water and food. She and Ishmael cried out to the Lord, and again the Lord responded to them. The Lord assured them of Ishmael's future as a great nation and opened their eyes to see a well close by. They continued to live in the wilderness, and Ishmael became an expert with the bow.

What a hard life Hagar had. But even though she was an Egyptian, she had a close relationship to God— as close of a relationship as Abraham and Sarah. This might show us that God is in our lives even when we haven't acknowledged Him ourselves. My sons and I have looked back on our lives before we came to Christ and are able to point out to each other things that happened to us that could only have been God.

Hannah: Mother of Samuel, Favored Wife of Elkanah

Hannah was another wife who was unable to conceive (1 Samuel 1:1–20). She was very desperate to have a child. Hannah prayed to God if He gave her a son, she would give her son to the Lord for all her son's life (1 Samuel 1:11–20). Eli, the priest, seeing her lips move, recognizing her desperation, and not hearing her speak out loud, accused her of being drunk. While she was drunk in the Lord, no alcohol had passed her lips (1 Samuel 1:15).

Peninnah, her husband's second wife, added to Hannah's problems. Elkanah, her husband, loved her dearly and claimed to be better to her than ten sons would be (1 Samuel 1:8). But Peninnah would give Hannah a hard time about being barren. The gracious Hannah would not fight back in words or deeds.

And while she kept her son until he was weaned (1 Samuel 1:22), she did uphold her promise and gave him to the Lord by leaving him with Eli the priest (1 Samuel 1:24–28). Like Mary, mother of Jesus, Hannah praised the Lord in prayer/song (1 Samuel 2:1–10).

Would I be able to leave my son to be raised by someone else? After waiting all that time for a child and not knowing if I would ever have another one, would I rationalize a reason to keep him near? I'd like to think I would obey. I am having trouble releasing my grandchildren. How would I ever leave my child on a permanent basis, even though she did see him yearly (1 Samuel 2:19)?

Later in the promise, would I want to take my son back after finding out I left my precious son with a man whose own sons were a mess (1 Samuel 2:12–26)? Would I question God's judgment about the qualifications of Eli? Or would I question if I understood God correctly?

This is the man I left my son to be cared for to raise my son to honor God? If his own sons are not honoring God and God is questioning Eli's focus, how could I not become unsure of the situation (1 Samuel 2:29)? God asks Eli why he (Eli) is honoring his sons more than he is honoring God?

Since there were no cell phones or computers back then, word traveled a lot slower. Hannah probably had no idea all those bad things were happening in Eli's family. Samuel is a prime example of no matter what is happening around us, God's wishes for us will prevail. Of course, it all worked out. Her son Samuel became a very important prophet, judge, and teacher who was mentioned many times in the Bible.

The Lord rewarded Hannah for her integrity and gave her three other sons and two daughters (1 Samuel 2:21).

Wives of other prominent men were also of great influence in a variety of ways.

Asenath: The wife of Joseph, Son of Jacob

Even though Joseph's brother sold him into slavery, eventually he was put in charge of all of Egypt. Joseph is an example of how despite all the things that happened to keep him from God's purpose in life, God's purpose will succeed in the end (Genesis 37, 39–41).

Pharaoh gave Joseph many things when he put Joseph in charge of Egypt (Genesis 41:44–45). One of the things Joseph received was a wife, Asenath, who was the daughter of Potiphera, a priest (Genesis 41:50). Since Asenath was not a Hebrew woman, Joseph should have refused to marry her. Pharaoh wanted to elevate Joseph's status by having him marry the daughter of a priest.

They had two sons, Manasseh and Ephraim (Genesis 46: 20), who were blessed by their grandfather Jacob and went on to become influential men in the promised land (Numbers 1:34–35). However, as influential as they became, their tribe did not flourish. Could that be because Joseph went against what God asked the Hebrews not to do (Ezra 9:12)? God asked that they not marry outside their faith.

I wonder what it felt like to be the wife of someone who had a past like Joseph. He landed on his feet in the end. From the daughter of an Egyptian priest came sons who became influential in the land of the Israelites. Jacob's blessing and Joseph's influence along with God's will, God did prevail.

Priscilla: Wife of Aquila, Friend of Paul's

They are never mentioned separately. It is always Aquila and Priscilla. As a couple, one with God, they are often referred to as the couple that best show what God meant a marriage to be like. There is never a mention of children in their lives. Along with their missionary lives, they were tent makers, as was Paul. Paul lived with them for eighteen months at one point.

Both of whom were missionaries on their own and with Paul. Paul would meet up with the couple, and they would work together (Acts 18:1–3). There were times when they could teach Paul things he did not know or understand (Acts 18:26). At other times they were on their own without Paul (Acts 18:18–19). They also spent time teaching Apollo (Acts 20:26).

Priscilla and Aquila were not always on the road as missionaries. They would also have a church in their home (1 Corinthians 16:16–19). Priscilla and Aquila seemed to be involved in the church, whether at home or in the field.

Both Paul (Romans 16:3–4) and Timothy (2 Timothy 4:19) at separate times greeted or mentioned the pair as an active part of their lives. As a couple, they were influencing others for God's kingdom. Priscilla must have had a great relationship with her husband since they lived and worked together. With the right mate, that continuous time together can be a blessing.

Abigail: Wife of Nabal and Later, Wife of David after Nabal's Death

Abigail's first husband, Nabal was not very intelligent and was a very surly, mean man. As a supporter of Saul, he did not like David. When asked by David to return a favor, Nabal refused (1 Samuel 25:1–39). This upset David to the point of wanting revenge.

While David and his men were on their way to kill Nabal's household, one of the servants let Abigail know what happened. Abigail, being just the opposite of her husband, intelligent, humble, and decisive, put a plan in action to ward off the impending war without telling her husband she was doing this.

She met David down the road before he could get to where Nabal was living and showed a most hospitable side of herself. David was doubly thankful to her because not only did he receive the gifts Abigail brought for his men and him, but she also kept David from having vengeful, needless bloodshed on his conscience.

When Abigail finally did tell the drunken Nabal what had happened, his heart failed, and ten days later he was dead. Nabal and Abigail are a prime example of being unevenly yoked (2 Corinthians 6:14). To Abigail's credit, she did not divorce Nabal. It was only after his death that she hooked up with David.

David had been so impressed with Abigail that when he heard that Nabal had died, David asked her to become his wife (1 Samuel 25:39–42). Abigail was protected by David and traveled with him at various times (1 Samuel 27:3, 30:5, 2 Samuel 2:2). David's second son, Kileab, or Daniel, was from Abigail (2 Samuel 3:3). She went from a fool for a husband to having a God-sanctioned king for a husband. It's always a good thing when you can trade up!

Bathsheba: Wife of Uriah and Later Wife of David after David Had Uriah Killed

David saw Bathsheba bathing on her roof and was smitten. He summoned Bathsheba to spend the night with him while her husband was away at war. She became pregnant (2 Samuel 11:1–5).

David ordered her husband, Uriah, to be killed in battle. Uriah did not sleep with his wife while home on leave from the battle that David arranged on purpose. David was hoping to use that leave time to say that the baby was Uriah's (2 Samuel 11:6–17). Since that did not work as David had planned, David arranged for Uriah's death in battle.

Bathsheba mourned the loss of her husband, but after the time of mourning was over, she became David's wife and gave him a son (2 Samuel 11:26–27).

But Bathsheba lost the baby that David had fathered while Uriah was still alive. David prayed and fasted over their dying child.

Even with the death of the child, David had not figured out how deeply he had sinned (2 Samuel 12:15–18). It took Nathan, the prophet, to come to David about the truth of David's sin to bring David and God back together again.

The Bible doesn't point out if Bathsheba knew about Uriah's death being part of David's plan or not. If she did know, I would wonder how that affected her relationship with David. Yes, he was a King. And he was favored by God. Further in their relationship when it was time for Solomon to become king, David listened to Bathsheba.

The Lord gave Bathsheba other children, and one of her sons was Solomon. Solomon was to become king after David, but one of David's other sons decided he was going to become king in place of Solomon. The prophet Nathan went to Bathsheba and alerted her as to what was happening without David's knowledge (1 Kings 1:11–31).

Bathsheba humbled herself before David. She was instrumental in attaining the role of king for Solomon. Without her effort, Solomon might never have become king.

Adonijah, who had tried to become king in place of Solomon, knew that Solomon listened to Bathsheba. When Adonijah wanted a certain woman as his wife, he asked Bathsheba for her help in making that happen. Adonijah knew that Solomon listened to Bathsheba, which told Adonijah how much power she held in the kingdom (1 Kings 2:13–21). Many wives and mothers throughout history have been the strength behind their husbands or sons. Bathsheba was prominent both with David and with Solomon.

One woman was honored because of being the daughter of a king and then becoming a wife of a king. You would think she had it all, but it didn't turn out that way.

Michal: Wife of David but also the Daughter of King Saul

During the time that God made Saul King, Michal was Saul's younger daughter (1 Samuel 14:49). Because David was always around at Saul's request, Michal could spend time around David (1 Samuel 18:20–28). She fell in love with David, and they wanted to be married.

The only requirement Saul had for David to accomplish before he would consent to the marriage was one hundred Philistine foreskins. When David accomplished that as asked, Saul began to fear David not only because of David's relationship with God but because of David's relationship with Michal (1 Samuel 19:11–17).

Saul's way of dealing with that fear was to try to kill David. Michal found out about the scheme and helped David to escape. Michal lied to and deceived her father (1 Samuel 25:44).

Saul, possibly out of spite because Michal gave assistance to David, gave Michal to Paltiel for his wife while David was not around to stop it (2 Samuel 3:13–16). Or was it Michal who wanted to move on to a husband who was possibly moving up the ladder of royalty? It depends upon what article I read as to which was the truth of Michal's involvement or not in her separation from David.

David wanted Michal back, so he set up his own scheme to have her taken from Paltiel. Because Paltiel cried and followed Michal to try to get her back, I must wonder if Michal and Paltiel had established a great marriage and that successful union was being interrupted by David.

Nothing is written that I could find about her shedding tears and wanting to stay with Paltiel. If they were as in love as Paltiel seemed to make us believe with his reaction to the loss of Michal, how would Michal have felt being taken away from Paltiel to return to David? Was she working more on her royal status? Or were the decisions being made without anyone asking her what she wanted to do?

At that time, most women had no say in their lives. I also had to ask myself why David wanted her back. Was it because he loved her so much and missed her, or was it for revenge against Saul (2 Samuel 6:16–23, 1 Chronicles 15:29)? So even though she was a daughter of a king, then the wife of a king, decisions were being made around her that she may not have been happy with. Or was she a great schemer, actress, and selfish woman?

At one point, David was celebrating the success of his effort in bringing back the ark of the Lord's to his city. He began to dance and leap about. Michal was embarrassed that he would act like that and "despised him in her heart" (2 Samuel 6:16). She chastised David for dancing and leaping.

Michal had no children to either of her husbands. What a roller coaster ride of a life for her. At that time and place, having no children brought shame to the woman. There was lots for Michal to cope with. She was now embarrassed for the man David had become, at least in her mind. Her own shame of having no children was always present. Then she had to adapt to leaving Paltiel to go back to her first husband. She must have had a miserable life.

This situation has reminded me of the Abbott and Costello dialog, "Who's on first?" If you remember this, your age is showing! If you don't remember it, Google it up on one of your devices. It will make you laugh!

Another reason women were acknowledged was because of the parents they came from. But in Dinah's case, she also wound up being a reason that a whole town of men were slaughtered. That was not her intention, but it was the way the situation ended.

Dinah: Daughter of Jacob and Leah

Dinah decided to go by herself to visit the local towns-women whom she didn't know. It was exciting to get out alone (Genesis 30:21). Was this in rebellion to decide to go alone? It was not a norm for this time. Or maybe someone dared her to go by herself.

One of the local men saw her and raped her (Genesis 34). But he loved her and wanted her as his wife. Dinah's brothers found out about the rape when the local man's father came to talk to Jacob about allowing Dinah to stay with his son. The local man's father was willing to do anything to keep Dinah as a wife for his son.

Dinah's brothers deceived the man's father. The brothers, without Jacob's knowledge, set the price for the bride. The brothers said that they could not give their sister to any man who was not circumcised, so all the men in that town agreed to be circumcised.

Three days after the circumcision when all of them were still sore, two of Dinah's brothers killed all the men of that town. And Dinah was returned to Jacob's family.

Think of what happens to Dinah during that era now that she had been with another man. No one would ever marry her now that she was defiled. (Although one of the articles I read stated that Dinah did get married.) And while she did not ask to be raped, it appears that the man fell in love with her. What were her feelings about him? She had remained with him after the rape.

It doesn't state, of course, what Dinah felt about her rapist or about returning to her family. Again, during this period of life, the woman's decision was often made for her. This time the decision was not even made by her father but by her two rebellious, angry brothers. Jacob did not know what his two sons had done until after it was all over.

What was in Dinah's head for the rest of her life knowing that a whole village of men were slaughtered because of a decision she made? She had no control over what her brothers did, but if she had not gone into town alone, this might not have happened. And in this place and time, single women did not go places alone. She did have control over her own actions. Did she regret that decision for the rest of her life? Was it worth her rebellion if that is why she did it?

Many of us have decisions we made in our past that we regret. After we repent, God has forgiven us those decisions. And maybe even the others affected by those decisions have forgiven us. But have we forgiven ourselves?

Often women who have come to me for counseling are still carrying the feeling of not being forgiven for their actions. We don't realize all the guilt, shame, and pain we are still carrying come from a lie from Satan. If we have asked for forgiveness, we know logically, in our brains, that He has forgiven us. But we are still unable to feel that forgiveness in our spirit. The enemy enjoys keeping us in his control and will keep us there for as long as we allow him to do that. More on forgiveness later.

Some women were acknowledged because they became queens. The most well known and loved by all, of course, was Esther. As mentioned earlier, she was created for such a time as this. In reality, so are we. God has us here and now for a reason. We may not save a specific group of people as she did. But whatever reason God has for putting us here is just as important to Him as Esther's calling. Other ladies who functioned as queens, good queens or bad queens, left an impression in history.

Vashti: First Queen to Xerxes

In a way, even though she was fired from her job as queen, she was one of a first "lady lib" examples because she would not obey the king (Esther 1:10). She would not allow herself to be degraded in front of other men.

Xerxes wanted to show her off to his drunken buddies. He wanted to parade her in front for all to see. She did not want to be treated that way and revolted. Women did not do that in that day. What a husband said, you obeyed, especially a king.

The king and his consultants were afraid if they allowed her to get away with this behavior, all the women of that kingdom would follow her. They could not allow that to happen, so she was fired as queen (Esther 2:17).

The hope of the king's consultants was that if Vashti was kicked out of her home, all the other women would not want that to happen to them. They felt with Vashti as an example, the rest of the women would continue to be submissive.

There is nothing written about where Vashti went, what happened to her afterward, or if she remained in the castles in the role of a lower woman. We can all agree that she certainly retained her integrity.

Athaliah: Queen to Jehoram, Mother of Ahaziah, then Ruler of Judah for Seven Years, Daughter of Jezebel

While Jehoram was king and Athaliah queen, the king had all his brothers and leaders killed (2 Chronicles 21:1–4). Therefore, the only person left to reign after Jehoram's death was his youngest son, Ahaziah.

Since Ahaziah was not married, his mother, Athaliah, became his adviser (2 Chronicles 22:1–9). His mother encouraged him to do wrong and follow the evil ways of the past. He ruled for one year. Jehu, who was the one appointed to kill all the family by Jehoram, caught up to Ahaziah and killed him too while he was in Samaria (2 Chronicles 22:7–9).

When Athaliah found out her son was killed, she destroyed the rest of the royal family. But a nurse responsible for Joash, the infant son of Ahaziah, protected and hid him for six years (2 Chronicles 22:10–12). Athaliah reigned seven long years.

For seven years all of Judah was ruled by a woman. No king was involved, just a queen. Unfortunately, she was not a good ruler. She did not honor God.

In the seventh year, Joash was crowned king. The revolt put Joash, the only surviving royal family member left, into place as king even though he was a child (2 Chronicles 23:1–11). The advisers to Joash had Athaliah killed. She was not to be killed in the temple but was killed where the horses entered the palace (2 Chronicles 23:12–15).

How disappointing it is that when we do finally get a woman in charge of the kingdom, she does such a horrible job. It would have been great if she would have been a strong leader, not only for Judah but for God's kingdom as well.

While we are talking evil here, let's look at some other evil women of the Bible.

Delilah: A Philistine and Samson's Downfall

This is another case of an angel showing up to a couple unable to conceive and preparing the way for a child who will greatly affect the kingdom of God in a positive way, at least at first. After the child Samson was born, his parents were given instructions as to how to raise him. He was to drink no wine or eat anything that was unclean. Also, he was never to have his hair cut because he was to be a Nazirite (consecrated to the service of God).

Samson's purpose was to rescue the Israelites from the Philistines (Judges 13:1–24). His strength had to do with his hair, which was never to be cut. Unfortunately, because he got mixed up with Delilah, a Philistine prostitute, he wound up being sidetracked from his purpose. She is sometimes referred to as the Judas of the Old Testament.

Samson enjoyed being with women (Judges 16:1–3). One day he fell in love with a woman named Delilah whom the Philistines had turned into a spy (Judges 16:14–22). Each time she asked him about his strength and where it came from, he would lie about it. Each time the Philistines tried to do to Samson the lie he had told Delilah that would harm him, they failed to subdue him. Finally, because of his desire to please her, and the fact that she had nagged him repeatedly, he shared the secret of his hair with her. She earned her money.

The Philistines captured him, cut his hair, gouged out his eyes, and made him a slave. Because his hair was cut, he became helpless. However, the Philistines never wondered what would happen when his hair started to grow back. They just thought they were safe.

But in the end, his strength came back with his hair, and he was able to kill a lot of Philistines and unfortunately himself all in the same maneuver. Even though Delilah turned spy against God to get money, she was not able to keep Samson from his purpose in the end. He rescued the Israelites by killing so many Philistines when he brought down the colosseum.

God always wins! No matter who or what the enemy puts in place to keep us from fulfilling our destiny, God will prevail. Samson is a prime example.

Jezebel: Queen and Wife of King Ahab

Ahab did what was evil in the eyes of God when he was king. And Jezebel fit right into that lifestyle (1 King 16:30–31, 18:3–5). Jezebel passed herself off as a prophet but supported those who honored Baal and Asherah, who were considered idol gods others worshiped instead of our Lord. Jezebel was killing off the Lord's prophets (1 Kings 18:4).

Elijah, who served the Lord, had killed all the prophets who were supported by Jezebel. She set her sights on killing Elijah (1 Kings 19:1–2). He ran away to hide, fearful that Jezebel would capture him and have him killed.

Here is yet another example of Jezebel not having an issue of killing whomever she wanted to get what she desired. This killing had to do with obtaining a garden for King Ahab that he really wanted (1 Kings 21:1–16). Jezebel had Naboth, the owner of the garden, set up as a man that cursed God and king. He was stoned to death so Ahab could have his garden.

But at one point the tables got turned on Jezebel (2 Kings 9: 7, 9:22). Jehu was anointed by God to avenge all the murders done to the Lord's prophets by killing the entire family of Ahab, which included Jezebel.

Jezebel's death was prophesied and delivered in a very horrible way (1 Kings 21:23–25, 2 Kings 9:30–37). She was thrown where horses trampled her, and her blood spattered the wall. Elijah had prophesied that Jezreel's dogs would devour Jezebel. Her body would be like dung, and no one would be able to identify her (2 Kings 9:30–37). There was not enough left of her to bury.

Often, even today, a woman may be referred to as a Jezebel when she represents herself as a prophet or a good person but leads particularly men astray to do her bidding. And her bidding is always evil bidding.

Jezebel's family was an example of how we can affect our families for generations by who we have become. Her daughter Athaliah was an evil queen, and Jezebel's grandson Ahaziah was an evil king. And those were the part of her family listed in the Bible. I am sure there were more family members who followed Jezebel's lifestyle.

For someone like me who has made bad decisions

at the beginning of my life, this shows the importance of repentance, obedience, and God's grace and mercy. I remember when I was making some of my bad decisions. I was thinking, *My bad decisions will affect only me, not my sons.* I gave myself permission to make those bad decisions because of that thought process.

Thankfully, my sons followed the Lord and were saved before I was. But Jezebel's family went the other way. Did it bother her in later life that her family members were leading evil lives? Or was she so evil that it didn't bother her that she was responsible for her daughter's and grandson's lives?

Sapphira: Wife of Ananias, Both Members of Jerusalem's Church

Ananias along with his wife, Sapphira, sold property (Acts 5:1–10). As was the procedure at that time, all assets were shared with that church group. When someone sold their land, whatever money they got went to a common pot in the church. Together, Ananias and Sapphira mutually made the decision as to how much money to give to the apostles and how much to keep for themselves. Ananias alone took the money for the church to the group.

Peter challenged Ananias, telling him not only did he lie to the church but to God. Ananias fell immediately to the ground dead. His body was removed and buried.

But they both had lied about how much they received for that property. Instead of giving the church what was due to the church, they decided to keep some for themselves. Unknown to Sapphira, her husband had already been before the apostles and lied about the amount of money.

However, she was given a chance to be honest. When asked about the amount of money they received for the property, she too lied. Peter also challenged her about lying to God. Peter remarked that her husband was already buried for his lie. Sapphira immediately dropped over dead, as her husband had earlier. She was buried beside her husband.

Are you asking yourself how Peter knew about the lies? While there can be different reasons that he knew, I prefer one above the rest. When we walk with God and help Him with His kingdom, He helps us in our kingdom. His help often includes the ability to sense when something is not right with God. For me, I lose my peace or get this uneasy feeling in my spirit (usually located about dead center of my abdomen).

One of my mentors always knew before I told her when I wasn't feeling well or when something was not right in my life. She would tell me that I was not feeling well today. One time she had to approach me about an accusation someone had made about me. It was not a good accusation. As she was continuing to explain the situation, she stopped talking before she got the whole experience explained to me.

She said, "Never mind. I can tell you had nothing to do with it."

I asked her to explain more about it to me because I was confused by what she was saying. She refused, saying, "No need. Let's move on." And so, we did. While I had been told who registered the complaint up front, I never heard the complete explanation about it. Like Peter, my mentor was given the gift of discernment.

The Bible shows examples of a *good woman* being used to show a *bad issue* and a *bad woman* being used as an example for a *good issue*. Let me explain through the next two women of the Bible.

Euodias: A Christian Woman

That's how she is listed if you research her name, so she could be every one of us. But in Philippians 4:2–3, we learn more about her. She had worked beside Paul for God's kingdom along with her friend Syntyche.

Here are two good Christian women who have worked hard for the good of God's kingdom who now seem to be fighting with each other within their church. They are disturbing the unity within that church.

Paul asked these ladies and an additional person (Epaphroditus, whom Paul had sent to the Philippian church, Philippians 2:25) to help with this situation. "I ask you, my true companion, help these women ..."

Unfortunately, any of us who are walking closely with our Lord can become distracted by the enemy. We wind up doing or saying some very non-Christian things. Often our pride gets in the way of our desire to right a wrong. Or it can be our stubbornness to hang on to something that deep inside we know is wrong or needs to be changed that allows the enemy his foothold.

We never find out if they did manage to stop fighting or if they continued. I like to think that at some point these ladies may have been involved in teaching other groups of women about God and that they used this past experience as a testimony for other women to learn how to recognize when the enemy is afoot.

We need to be aware that we are under attack from Lucifer and destroying friendships that work well for God's kingdom are targets for God's enemy. But we can take charge of Satan and not allow him to negatively affect what God has already anointed for His kingdom.

Here God has used good people to show that we can all fall at any time but also that God will provide help or a way to turn whatever is bad around again to good.

Gomer: A Promiscuous Woman

Gomer is quite the opposite title compared to Euodias. The prophet Hosea was instructed by God to marry a promiscuous woman (Hosea 1:1–9). Can you imagine what the people must have been thinking about Hosea as a prophet marrying Gomer?

God was trying to show the Israelites living in Jezreel how far they had fallen away from Him. God was no longer going to show this group of Israelites love or forgiveness or that they were any longer His people.

The first three children born of Hosea and Gomer were given names with specific negative meanings to deliver God's message to these lost people. First was a son named Jezreel to remind the Israelites of a massacre at Jezreel and that God was going to "break Israel's bow in the valley of Jezreel" (Hosea 1:5).

The first daughter was named Lo-Ruhamah, which means not loved, to show that God had no love of Israel. The third child was a son named Lo-Ammi, which means not my people. He was telling them He was no longer their God.

How awful for Gomer if she was trying to become a better person since she had married up. As father and mother of these three, it had to bother them that their children were being labeled and used as they were. But Hosea obeyed the Lord. No wonder Gomer ran away from home to live with another man.

However, at one point the Lord told Hosea to go show love to his wife even though she was with someone else (Hosea 3:1–5). Again, God used Gomer as an example to the Israelites. Hosea taking back Gomer and loving her equated to God taking back the Israelites and loving them. It is not listed, that I could find, how Gomer responded to Hosea wanting her back. Hopefully she could love Hosea back after he showed her forgiveness and love.

Here was a bad person being used to try to show a group of people that they needed to do good instead of evil. When I think about how this story played out, I must wonder about something. Did the people realize what was really going on at the time?

I know that I miss understand or don't pay attention enough to get everything I should get out of a situation while it is happening. At times, I must stand back later and look at what transpired. Only then do I get what I was supposed to get while it was occurring. Hopefully Hosea, Gomer, and the Israelites did a better job of figuring things out than I do at times.

I need to interject here with some personal information. For several years before I was saved, I was living in the fetish world. I lived within a world so opposite of God's kingdom that honored Satan—the world of bondage, latex clothing, and pornography. Not only did I live in it, but it was also my means of financial support.

Even though I wasn't saved at the time, occasionally I would pause and say, "Lord, this can't be a right way to live." Yet we were doing very well financially, and within this culture, we were respected businesspeople.

I kept fooling myself that if God were against this, He would not have made us as successful as we were.

After turning my life around, getting saved, and becoming active in my Christian life, I was ashamed of my past. I had only shared my past with a few people. It hurt me to even think about the world I left behind and who I had become. It hurt me to think how much I had hurt God during this time away from Him. I eventually could share all my past with one of my mentors/counselors and find God's forgiveness, mercy, and grace.

No matter how far away from God you feel you are at this moment, if He took me back, as He did Gomer, He will welcome you too. More about this concept later in this book.

One day I was at a woman's conference at my church. A lady from the church who was part of the presenters and who had never laid eyes on me before was prophesying over me. In general, this is what she told me: "You have spent a time in your life living a lifestyle that you were not comfortable in. God wants you to know that He placed you there for a reason. That experience is going to help you fulfill something within your future calling. Do not be ashamed. God was with you even then."

A few years later, after proper training, is when I started my counseling ministry. I quickly learned that by sharing my testimony of who I was then in comparison to who I was sitting before them now, it would allow them to share things with me they had never shared with anyone else in their lives.

They knew they could be open and honest with me about their lives and I would not judge them or chastise them. The seventy-two-year-old pillar of the church lady could confess her past life to me and be released from her shame. She could find forgiveness and rejoice in a freedom she had never felt before by making herself right with God.

After I heard that prophecy, instead of being ashamed, I could turn those feeling around to thank God for that time in my life. It provided me with a way to have my clients identify with me instead of being afraid to tell "a good Christian" what "bad things" they had done in the past. God took what Satan meant for harm and turned it around and used it for His kingdom!

If you have a hidden past, I pray that you find someone you can be open and honest with as well. There is a level of joy and freedom out there from your creator just waiting for you to receive it. He has forgiven you a long time ago. But until we forgive ourselves and no longer allow the enemy to put us in a place of shame, we will not feel inside us that level of goodness God meant us to have when He created us. Do not allow Satan access to that part of you any longer than you must!

When I tell you that *You Are Today's Women of the Bible*, here is a prime example. I can identify with Gomer as well as some other women of the Bible. How about you? Have you found yourself in one or more of the women of the Bible? If not, here are some more women to use as comparisons.

Earlier we separated out the Mary's. It's time to do the same thing for the Tamar's. The first Tamar we will look at is one of the first woman's lib stories in the world. She didn't just sit back and allow the Lion of Judah to take advantage of her. She protected herself and her future.

Tamar Number One: The Daughter-in-Law of Judah

Judah married and had three sons. Two sons were close in age. The third son was further behind in his arrival. When son number one was ready to marry, he married Tamar (Genesis 38:6–26).

Son number one was wicked. The Lord put him to death before he and Tamar could have a child. Judah told son number two, "It's time for you to step up and marry Tamar." He was instructed not only to marry her but also to produce a child. That child would be credited to son number one.

Son number two did marry Tamar as instructed by his father. However, son number two did not want to have a child with her that would not be considered his. So, he cheated in the sexual act department (Genesis 38:9). He never allowed his semen to enter Tamar. Birth control was born to the world, but no child was born. The Lord put him to death also. Judah told Tamar to go home to her family until son number three was older.

Time went by, and Judah did not call Tamar back into the family. She realized that Judah was cheating her out of her place in his family. She learned that Judah was heading into town to take care of some business.

Tamar dressed herself up as a prostitute, and Judah slept with her. Since he didn't have payment available for her services, he gave her his seal, cord, and staff as collateral until he could get the payment to her. She did not hang around to receive that payment. When Judah sent one of his men to town with her payment, Tamar was nowhere to be found.

She was pregnant with Judah's child. About three

months later, Judah was informed by the family that Tamar must have turned herself into a prostitute. She was now pregnant. Judah declared that Tamar was no longer an honorable woman. She was to be stoned.

When she presented herself to the family, she had her own story to tell about her pregnancy. Tamar showed all the items she had been given from the man that got her pregnant. All were in shock, most of all, Judah. She was never stoned.

Judah did declare in a later statement that Tamar was a better person than he was. He had intended to cheat her out of son number three. Since she was carrying Judah's child, she was accepted into the family. As it turned out, she was carrying twin boys. Tamar was taken care of for the rest of her life. She bore two of the five sons of Judah.

Two things about this story are interesting. Judah, the Lion of Judah, was a great man in many ways according to other parts of the Bible (Genesis 43, 49, Judges 1). But he fell prey to the enemy and sinned just as easily and quickly as any of us could do. This story shows how the enemy can attack someone strong in the word of God just as easily as someone who is not walking with God. So, watch your back. The devil is sneaky!

Second, Tamar stood up for herself in an era when that did not happen. Women's lives were planned by men in the family. She was not going to be taken advantage of by this man even though he was one of the big shots of his era.

One of my single ladies had a hard time taking care of herself in a situation. A husband and wife whom she had known for years contacted her because the wife was dying. She helped care for this wife until her death. The husband called less than a month after the death and asked to take her to dinner as a thank-you for the care of his wife.

However, without asking permission, he grabbed my lady and pulled her to him in a passionate on-the-mouth kiss. He did it a second time at her home after he took her home. She was so surprised each time that she did nothing.

A few days later, she asked me to help compose a letter to him (she does not own a computer) to tell him she never wanted to see him again. He had called her wanting to get more hugging and kissing time with her.

Being a strong Christian woman, she was trying to be gentle and nice in the wording she had composed. The only problem with that is it did not in no uncertain terms tell him to stay away. She felt she couldn't get strong with him without hurting him.

I reminded her about what Jesus did at the temple when He found men that were using his temple as a place of business. They were selling items and making money (Matthew 21:12–13). He made them understand in no uncertain terms that they were to leave.

Ladies, if you find yourself in a situation that makes you uncomfortable and you need to make yourself known as to how you feel about what is happening to you, say it. You don't need to swear or used off terms or language. But you do need to protect God's temple, which is you. He lives inside of you in the form of the Holy Spirit.

Protect your temple just as Jesus protected His (1 Corinthians 6–19).

Tamar Number Two: The Daughter of David, Sister of Absalom and Amnon

There was a second younger brother to Tamar by the name of Amnon. Amnon was sick with want for Tamar as more than a sister. His adviser was his uncle. This man was uncle to Absalom and Tamar as well. Still the uncle told Amnon how to get Tamar into his life with no consideration of what this would do to her.

Amnon would have to play a trick on David (2 Samuel 13:1–32). He was to act very sick so that his father, David, would come to see Amnon. Then Amnon asked David to send his sister Tamar to him as his nurse/cook. David agreed. Tamar cooked the meal in front of Amnon as he asked her to do. When she was finished, he asked her to bring the food over to him in his bed. Again, Tamar did as ask.

A healthy Amnon tried to rape her. She resisted. Tamar gave him lots of other options, one of which was to ask David for permission to marry. Amnon refused all the other options and forced himself on her.

The minute the sexual act was over, Amnon hated Tamar. He had her thrown out of his house. That meant that no one would ever marry her because she was violated. No one would support her for the rest of her life.

Absalom, her brother, found her out in the street after the rape. She told him what happened. He instructed her to keep it to herself. Tamar was not to tell others. Absalom took her in, and she lived the rest of her life as part of his house.

When David heard the story, he was furious but did nothing about it. Great parenting! *Not!* Absalom hated Amnon for the rest of Amnon's life, which wasn't long. Two years later (2 Samuel 13:23), Absalom killed

Amnon. Could David have prevented this death if he would have handled the situation when it happened?

Tamar's life was ruined. Second Samuel 13:20 says she lived a desolate woman even though she was technically cared for by her brother, Absalom.

I realize that in that era there was little Tamar could do about her situation. And I realize as a survivor of rape myself that my feelings are tainted. There was a time that I blamed myself for not fighting back harder. Like Tamar, I was physically overpowered as a child by adult males. Eventually I put that all into proper prospective and knew I was not at fault and there was nothing I could do at the time.

My spirit hurts miserably for any of the Tamar's out there who have not found peace from a past unpleasant experience—those who have decided to keep it in, just not deal with it. If I leave it alone, it will go away—eventually.

I can't say it loud enough, often enough, or adamantly enough: there is a freedom waiting for you to open yourself to receive from your Creator. There are counselors, mentors, or advisors trained to help you find that freedom. You may not realize the desolate life you are living inside because of someone else who took advantage of you.

Some of my ladies who have come to me because of their own sexual abuse didn't realize the desolation they were living with until the freedom was achieved. But I know deep, deep inside you, you know things are not right. The fight for your freedom is well worth that fight.

But you must be willing to step into the ring and put on your boxing gloves, in the form of God's armor

(Ephesians 6:13–18). You can do it! Don't wait another day. Make that call. Take that step. You are worth it.

Tamar Number Three: Daughter of Absalom

It appears that Absalom was still feeling bad about what Amnon did to their sister Tamar. Absalom cared so much about his wronged sister that he named his only daughter Tamar (2 Samuel 14:27).

I can only guess that Tamar number three was named for her aunt, Tamar number two, although it does not state that in the Bible. Absalom killed Amnon, and that was not good. He cared for his sister for life, and that was good. Not only did Absalom take care of her for her entire life, but he also possibility named his daughter after her. The Bible states that Tamar number three "became a beautiful woman."

I hope she made her aunt proud! I can just see Tamar number two holding, cuddling, and maybe spoiling Tamar number three. Tamar number three may have been a gift from God to Tamar number two. Tamar number two would never marry and have children of her own. But I would guess that she might help raise her nephews and nieces.

While I love my grandsons with every fiber of my being, there is something special about my granddaughter in a special corner of my heart. I have a picture of each of us about the age of five years old. We look so much alike that when I showed the picture of me to my grandsons, her brothers, they thought it was her.

My grandsons will joke about my granddaughter being my favorite, but I told them they got extra Christmas presents because of her. I would be done with my shopping and then find something I just had to get her. Therefore, to keep the number of presents equal, I had to go out and buy each of them one more.

I hope that Tamar number two in her own way found something special in her life because of her relationship with Tamar number three.

We come to a list of women who became famous because they were strong, successful women. They stood on their own merit and not because of whom they begot, wed, or were born to. We start with two Deborah's.

Deborah: Nursemaid to Rebekah and Later Nursemaid to Jacob and Esau

When Rebekah decided to marry Isaac, she was released from her family to travel to Isaac's family. Deborah was Rebekah's nursemaid. As was done in that time, Deborah's life was dictated by the men in the family. She was sent to Isaac's family along with Rebekah (Genesis 24:59, 61).

Deborah was later nursemaid to Jacob and Esau. This makes her influential in the development of men who would rule nations. The Lord entrusted her to help raise some of His children who would be instrumental in affecting His kingdom.

Deborah lived a long time and was buried under an oak tree while Jacob was traveling to Bethel (Genesis 35:6–8).

She must have been important to the family. After all the children were grown, Deborah was not dismissed from the family. She continued to travel with them, and to have her death and burial mentioned in the Bible must show her importance in Jacob's family's lives. To my knowledge, the death and burial of

Mary, the mother of Jesus, is not listed anywhere in the Bible. But Deborah's is listed.

Deborah: Prophetess, Warrior, and Only Female Judge in Premenarchial Israel

First, she became a wife, a prophetess, and a judge in Israel (Judges 4:4–5). Her courtroom was under a palm tree. Deborah called Barak to become a warrior and go into battle. She gave him battle plans promising Barak that God would deliver success in those battles. But Barak refused to go unless Deborah went with him (Judges 4:8–10).

Deborah agreed to go into battle with Barak but foretold that because of Barak's decisions, the honor of the war would not be his. God would deliver Sisera, the leader of Jabin's army, into the hands of a woman. Her prophecy came true. See Jael.

As a warrior along with Barak, she continued to lead the way in Israel's war. She and Barak were victorious as God had promised (Judges 4:14). Her faith in God to provide on His promise strengthened Barak for him to do his job.

Deborah and Barak returned from war singing to the Lord (Judges 5:1–12). She was heralded as "a mother in Israel" who "arose" to victory over the enemies of Israel (Judges 5:7).

What a mixture this woman was. The Bible never mentions biological children even though she is listed as a mother to Israel. With all her strengths, what was her relationship with her husband? To be a woman and judge in this era was very rare.

A woman as a warrior was an additional rarity in her time. She fought beside men, led men, and followed God's direction during her time in battle. Her strength as a warrior was only outdone by her commitment to God.

She was also a writer. The song she sang after the battle was hers. Was there anything this woman couldn't do? I wonder who did the cooking and the laundry.

There were other strong women who saved the day in battle. God revealed their calling to them, and they obeyed. Would we do as well?

Jehosheba: Saved Joash, Who Would Become King

When Queen Athaliah decided to destroy all King Ahaziah's family, Jehosheba took Ahaziah's infant son, Joash, and stole him away (2 King 11:2–4). The rest of the children were all killed, but Joash and a nurse were hidden in a bedroom and saved. Joash was hidden in a temple for six years until he became king at a very young age.

Jehosheba was Ahaziah's sister. What a great aunt to have on your side. Had she failed, the line of Judah would have ended. She was also the only princess to marry a high priest.

I am sure Jehosheba really had no idea of how important it was to save Joash. She did not sit there and say, "I need to save Joash or the line of Judah will cease to exist. And if I do this, some day when they write a book about all this, I will be listed in it as a heroine."

You are not sitting there saying, "Since I decided to stay home and raise my children and support my husband, someday I will be listed in history as the mother who raised my daughter who will save the world from starvation in the year 2060." But the bottom line is we have no idea how our decisions, our influence, will affect the world or God's kingdom in the future. If they write another Bible, how will I be listed?

Jael: Heroine Who Killed Sisera, Which Helped Deliver Israel from Its Enemy

Sisera was commander of Jabin's army, the enemy of Israel (Judges 4:7). He was about to be handed over to Deborah and Barak. But Sisera escaped on foot (Judges 4:15). He fled on foot right into the tent of Jael (Judges 4:17–22).

Jael recognized Sisera but was accommodating to him. Feeding him and standing in the doorway to protect him, she inherited his trust. Sisera felt safe and exhausted, falling asleep in the tent.

Jael picked up a tent spike and a hammer. She went quietly to Sisera and drove a spike into his temple and killed him. About that time, Barak showed up. Jael announced what she had done. Her actions became part of the song Deborah and Barak sang while returning from the war (Judges 5:24–27).

Scripture mentions that Jael had a husband whose family was in alliance with Jabin, the enemy (Judges 4:17). However, scripture doesn't mention that her husband was present at the time she killed Sisera. This might have been good for Israel. Jael's husband probably would not have allowed her to kill Sisera. In this time, women often only did what their husbands told them to do. They often did not make decisions on their own. Jael didn't hesitate and killed Sisera.

I had to wonder why Jael chose that method of murder. Online information explains that she obviously lived in a tent. Back then, women were proficient with putting up, taking down, and taking care of the tent. She would have been extremely comfortable with a tent spike and hammer. Plus, it would have been an instrument of convenience. She would have had tent spikes available easier than a knife or a sword.

Don't you wonder what the discussion sounded like at dinner that night? "Hi, honey, welcome home. How was your day? Oh, by the way, I drove a spike into Sisera's head today. You know him, Jabin's army commander. I killed him here in this tent, right where you are standing. Deborah and Barak stopped by. Said hi. Dinner's ready. Are you hungry?'

Rahab: Prostitute in Jericho Who Became Part of the Lineage of Jesus

According to Rabbinic literature, Rahab was a manu-facturer of dyed linen as well as her role as a harlot. It also states that she was converted to Christianity at the age of fifty. After her conversion, she married Joshua, birthing Jeremiah, Hilklah, Seraiah, Mahseiah, and Baruch. That's an awful lot of birthing after the age of fifty. Miracles do happen.

However, in Matthew 1:5–16, she is credited with marrying Salmon of the tribe of Judah and became the mother of Boaz, which of course eventually led to the birth of Jesus. There are a lot later-in-life births in that era compared to today.

Joshua 2 tells the complete story of how Rahab, a prostitute, started the process that eventually led her to become part of the genealogy of Jesus Christ (Matthew 1:5). Joshua had sent two spies to Jericho. Even after the king of Jericho demanded that she turn in the spies, she hid them on her roof. Then she lied, telling the king that the spies had been there but had left by a certain route.

After the king's men left, Rahab admitted to the

spies her fear of their God. She had heard about their God and wanted to make a deal. Rahab had protected them, so she wanted protection for her family. She wanted protection when their God took control of Jericho, as He had done with other cities.

The spies gave her a game plan and told her to gather her family into her home. She was to place a scarlet cord in the window to mark her home for the attacking armies. The promise would hold only if she continued to keep the scout's secret, which of course she did.

The spies told the attacking men from Joshua's troops to avoid attacking the house with the scarlet cord (Joshua 6:17–25). Rahab and her family were the only survivors. Jericho's walls came tumbling down, and the city was burned to the ground.

Rahab is mentioned again in Hebrews 11:31 and James 2:25. She was one of the people who proved their faith in God by their deeds. Rahab was compared to Abraham as another example of faith and deeds.

If she can move from prostitute to part of the family of Jesus, you and I can also be forgiven for our sins. It doesn't matter who we were before we ask for forgiveness. Once we are redeemed, God will want to put us to work. With His grace and mercy, we can become active in God's kingdom as one of His ambassadors! Have you taken that step yet? See the next chapter on salvation.

As Rahab became a part of the lineage of Christ, so have others become related to Jesus.

Ruth: A Moabite, Daughter-in-Law of Naomi, Wife of Boaz (Ruth 4:21–22), and Therefore, a Part of the Genealogy of Jesus.

The book of Ruth starts out with Naomi, who loses her husband and both her sons. The sons had married Moabite women, which meant they were not necessarily honoring our God.

Because food was scarce, Naomi decided to go back to Bethlehem, to go back home. She told her daughters-in-law of this decision. While she loved them both dearly, she released them to return to their own families in Moab. Orpah agreed to go home, but Ruth did not.

Ruth declared her love for Naomi, and where Naomi went, Ruth went. Whatever Naomi ate, Ruth ate. And whichever God Naomi honored, Ruth now honored also (Ruth 1:16). Ruth wished to care for Naomi.

In Bethlehem, where they moved, Ruth hung out close to a grain field and picked up the leftovers after the field hands were through. The field was owned by Boaz, who was a relative of Naomi's deceased husband. Boaz had heard about Ruth, who had decided to care for Naomi. And he felt somewhat indebted to her because of her decision to care for Naomi.

He told Ruth she was to pick along with his crew and when she was thirsty, she was to get a drink (Ruth 2:8). Boaz also told his workers to favor Ruth. Naomi decided she should find a husband for Ruth and Boaz looked like a great catch. She instructed Ruth in a way to flirt with Boaz, Jesus's day style, which was far different than today (Ruth 3:7–15).

Boaz was smitten. However, there were some things Boaz had to do first to claim Ruth. The knight-in-shining-armor won the battle for the fair maiden, and they were married. They had a son, Obed. Naomi became the nurse maid to Obed and found a new life for herself.

Obed was the father of Jesse and Jesse the father of David and on to Christ Jesus. By Ruth doing the right thing, to decide to care for her mother-in-law, she placed herself in line for blessings and look how it all ended! She was an ancestor of Jesus Christ.

Being the mother of two sons, I can attest to the importance of the mother-in-law, daughter-in-law relationship. I love my sons, and they love me. But there is a woman-to-woman bond established between my daughters-in-laws and me. There are times I am sure that I drive them nuts, after all it's in a mother-in-law's job description. Yet in a special corner of my heart, there is love reserved just for them.

There were some other women of the Bible who became entrepreneurs, CEOs, or leader types, which in that day was far from a typical role for a woman.

Lydia: One of the First Converts in Philippi and an Early Successful Businesswoman

She was a dealer in purple cloth and had opened her heart to Paul's message about the Lord (Acts 16:14–15). She would spend time out of her business day to go to the riverside and listen to the preaching. Lydia invited Paul and his group to come and stay at her home.

When Paul and Silas came out of prison, Lydia's house was their first stop when they were set free (Acts 16:40). She was not ashamed to have prisoners staying at her home. Often, she had other missionaries staying at her home

As someone who dealt in purple cloth, which was indicative of wealth and status, Lydia was considered an active and successful businesswoman. There is no mention of a husband in her life, yet she owned a home and had servants. Obviously, not only did she support herself but servants and guest alike.

Lydia must have had some wealth herself to invite not just Paul but all his followers who were actively participating in the baptism of herself and her household. She was not a Christian when she first met Paul, but she became a very active Christian. In some of the research I read, she is credited with having the first church in Philippi in her home.

Miriam: Moses and Aaron's Sister, Poetess, and Prophetess

Miriam took on the role of protector for Moses early in her life (Exodus 2:4–8). They were killing boy babies because of Pharaoh's rules. But Miriam's mom saw something special in her son Moses. (Don't we all?) She placed him in a basket and sent Moses floating down the river in hopes of someone rescuing Moses that he might live. Miriam was sent to walk along the river to protect Moses as best she could.

When Pharaoh's daughter decided to care for the baby, Miriam offered to summon a woman from the village to nurse the three-month-old infant. That provided the opportunity for Moses's mother to care for him until he was weaned. Not only did she get to nurse him, but she was paid for it on top of that.

Depending upon different articles, Miriam is listed as remaining single or married to Hur. Either way, after being separated from Moses for forty years, she and Aaron became important in Moses's role to free the Israelites.

At the point in their travels when Pharaoh's horses

and men fell into the Red Sea, Miriam (Exodus 15:20–21) took up a musical instrument and stirred the woman to dance and sing praises to the Lord, again supporting or influencing others for the good of Moses's cause and establishing herself as a leader.

Unfortunately, as in all families, there came a time when Miriam, along with Aaron, talked against Moses (Numbers 12). Miriam became jealous of Moses's leadership and relationship to God. The Lord called all three of them outside their tent and descended as a cloud. He chastised Aaron and Miriam.

When the cloud lifted, Aaron noticed Miriam had become a Leper. Moses was anguished at this and asked the Lord to heal her. For seven days, she needed to be isolated from the group until she was healed. The group of Israelites did not move on until those seven days passed.

This incident seemed to change Miriam. We don't find anything else about her in the Bible until her death. When Miriam died (Numbers 20:1), she was buried in the Desert of Zin. She was honored in her death but died so close to the time of the Promised Land.

Later, as the Lord was reminding the Israelites of the things He had done for them, He honored Miriam by reminding them that He had provided her as one of their leaders along with Moses and Aaron (Micah 6:4). While not perfect, and who is, Miriam was a strength behind Moses and Aaron's success.

There are various things we can learn from Miriam. While she was given power, she craved more. Her jealousy of Moses's power caused her to allow the enemy into her spirit. It shows how easily those of us who walk close to God can still make mistakes. We can, without realizing it, change our lives to the point of sin that allows the enemy to affect our way of life and personalities. That doesn't mean, though, that we can't fight back to regain our positions again. Look at David.

When she and Aaron revolted against Moses, I must wonder if she wasn't the instigator instead of Aaron. She is the one that became a leper, not Aaron. As a leader, she would have the power to lead for the enemy just as much as she had power to lead for the Lord.

Moses gives us a lesson in forgiveness here. Even with the trouble that Miriam caused, Moses asked God to heal his sister. At Moses's request, she was healed but certainly changed. Unlike David, who rallied after his fall with Bathsheba, Miriam fell back into obscurity. It saddens me to see a strong, successful woman like Miriam give up if indeed she did.

Should you find yourself in the place of making a mistake along the road following the Lord, fight, fight, fight to reclaim your position in God. Do not let the enemy win by changing you into passivity as he did with Miriam. Get back to being God's cheerleader! It won't be easy, but it will be worth it!

Huldah: Prophetess—King Josiah Sent Men to Huldah for Advice

Huldah lived in Jerusalem and was known as a prophet. Several priests and men went to speak with her. She told the men of the disaster God was going to bring to Jerusalem because the people were honoring other gods instead of Him (2 Kings 22:14–20, 2 Chronicles 34:22–28).

But to the king of Judah she sent another message. Because the king had humbled himself before God when he realized what was happening, the disaster would not occur until after Josiah's death. He would not have to live through the disaster because of his repentance.

The king relied on a woman to influence him as to what was to happen in his own kingdom and to him personally. She was used other times in the Bible as a prophetess according to various articles online.

Some women of the Bible were known as those who fought for the rights of others or for themselves.

Hogla, Noah, Tirzah, Milcah, and Mahlah: Five Daughters of Zelophehad Who Fought for Property Rights

Zelophehad had no sons, only daughters (Numbers 36:1–13). At that time, only sons could inherit land. With no money or land, the daughters would become destitute, so those daughters fought for their dad's property after his death.

Moses went to God for the answer. The Lord gave him an answer. God has always found a way to provide for orphans and widows. While these were adult or older daughters at the time, they were still orphans.

The daughters won the fight, but it had a contingency attached to it. They could not marry outside of their clan. The property could not be transferred to another clan or someone outside of the Israelite nation.

All five daughters married cousins on their father's side and stayed within their clan.

There was a new precedent set because of these daughters. Who could inherit was reworked, and a new law was established. This new law may well have affected many of us. I know it has me. When my father died, both my brother and I inherited what he wanted

us to have. I would have been left out of the will if
these daughters had not fought for me!

Puah and Shiphrah: Two Midwives Who Saved Hebrew Newborn Boys

The king of Egypt told the midwives, "When you are
delivering babies, if it is a girl, let it live. If it is a boy,
kill it" (Exodus 1:15–22). But the midwives loved the
Lord and refused to do that.

The king called them in and asked what was happening that the boy babies were still living. Puah
and Shiphrah told the king that Hebrew women were
stronger than Egyptian women and that often the
baby was born before they arrived, or at times they
were not used at all.

God honored the women for doing that by giving
them their own families.

I am quite sure where these ladies would land
today on the topic of abortion. As gutsy as they were
then to the king of Egypt, what would they do today
with our social media availability?

A Greek Mother: Syrophoenician Woman of Faith.

The woman was Greek born in Syrian Phoenicia (Mark
7:24–30, Matthew 15:21–28). Her daughter was possessed by a demon. The Greek mother came to Jesus
and fell at His feet asking for help to heal her daughter.

At first, He refused her, saying, "It is not right to
take the children's bread and throw it to the dogs."
Basically, He was saying, "You are not a Jew, so I don't
owe you any gifts as I do those who honor Me."

But the Greek mother pushed on for her daughter
and responded, "But even dogs under the table eat the

children's crumbs." Because of her persistence and faith in Jesus to heal her daughter, Jesus sent her home to her healed daughter. The demon was gone.

Achsah: Asked for Land, Then for Water for That Land, Took Care of Herself

Achsah was won by Othniel as part of a gift from her father (Joshua 15:15–19, Judges 1:9–13). She wanted her husband to ask for land from Caleb, but he did not ask. Since he would not ask, she did. Not only did she ask for land but water rights to support that land, ensuring her family would be able to take care of themselves.

As a wife and at some point, expecting to be a mother, she took over, at least for this instance, in support of her family. We want our husbands to be head of the household, but we don't always get a husband who is willing or able to do that. There is still a way to be more assertive when needed and still honor our husbands. By treating our husbands with the respect due to them, we are honoring God.

The last of the women of the Bible listed in this book are a group of individuals who did something odd and curious, interesting, or just cute.

Abishag: Kept David Warm—and That's All

While Abishag is listed as a concubine of David's, she never had sexual relations with him (1 Kings 1:1–4). David was dying and unable to keep warm. She was hired to take care of him, including to lay with him to keep him warm.

The Bible talks about her beauty, but I must wonder what her beauty had to do with her ability to take care of him and keep him warm. Maybe back then, pretty women had better circulation than ugly women!

Rhoda: Servant Girl Who Slammed the Door in Peter's Face When He Came out of Prison.

When Peter got out of prison unexpectedly, he went to Mary, mother of John Mark's house. The servant girl Rhoda answered the door. She was so overjoyed, she slammed the door shut in Peter's face and ran back into the house to tell all Peter was at the door. They didn't believe her.

Did they not believe her because it was impossible for him to be free, or was it impossible that she would have slammed the door in his face? I am sure it was the former, but I am guessing the latter was unbelievable also.

Mahalath: Either Had Bad Luck or Lost Blessings from the Lord.

Mahalath had two not-so-great things as part of her generational inheritance. First, she was the daughter of Ishmael, who was not the favored son of Abraham (Genesis 28:9). Second, not only was she the wife of Esau, who was the not favored some of Isaac, but she was his third wife (Malachi 1:2–3).

This poor woman couldn't catch a break. Hopefully there were lots of blessings for her from her heavenly Father that were not listed in the Bible.

Sometimes we feel like we can't catch a break. It feels like all is going wrong in our lives and it's hard to find the blessings or feel God's presence. But He is there. And there are blessings. We just must pay closer attention and look harder. Changing our attitudes or the way we are looking at something is hard to do but will help us adjust our lives for the better.

When life is the hardest, that is when God will look to see if we run toward Him or away from Him. His arms are always open.

Salome: Daughter of Herodias, Danced for Herod

Salome was either a good dancer or Herod was so drunk anyone would look good (Matthew 14:1–12, Mark 6:14–29). Either way, he was so impressed with her dance he told her she could have anything she asked for up to half his kingdom.

Not sure what to ask for, she went to her mother for advice. Her mother, Herodias, hated John the Baptist because he had spoken out against her marriage (Matthew 14:3). John the Baptist, being in prison already, was available to Herodias and her hate. She told her daughter to ask for John the Baptist's head on a platter.

While the king was hesitant to do this, knowing the discord it would create in the crowds, he had no choice. It was done.

Salome was in a hard place. We don't know what her own thoughts were about John the Baptist. But often children do get into a situation where they don't know what to do. It becomes difficult to obey their parent and do what they think is just if the parent and child are of a different mind. In their head, they may know that it is God they should listen to above the parent, but acting on that logic can be very difficult. Have you ever been there?

There are names that come in and out throughout the Bible, like Joanna and Susana who support Jesus and the disciples. And there may be others you are curious about in their roles in the Bible. But what you cannot deny is that women were part of God's plan for His created world. And that is still true today.

If they were going to write an addendum to the Bible a thousand years from now, who do you think they would be writing about? *You!*

You can't tell me Mary Magdalene sat back after she told the disciple that Jesus had risen and has this thought: *I wonder when they write the Bible in the future, will my name be in it?*

Do you think Lois and Eunice sat around having tea saying, "Since we decided to give up our professions to stay home and raise Timothy, they better put our names in the Bible when they write it. Look at all we gave up for God's kingdom."

Not all mentioned in the Bible are people who influenced thousands. Yes, some were. But many have minor roles. Some are listed with no name because at the time, the act they were participating in appeared to be so minor no one got their name. But when God sat down the writers of the Bible, He wanted those nameless people put in.

You may think what you did yesterday for that neighbor who is in need is nothing. Yet because that neighbor saw God in what you did, you will have no idea how that story will affect her grandchild when she tells that story to him. He takes that story in his spirit long after you have gone on to heaven and affects thousands because of your deed to his grandmother.

Let's go, ladies! Let's live each day as if whatever we are doing is going to show up in the addendum to the Bible being written long after we are already in heaven.

We are today's women of the Bible!

2

What Is Salvation? Are You Saved?

W hat do you think is going to happen to you when you die? Can you say for sure that you will go to heaven? How many times have you heard others talk about being saved? Or the question, "Do you think she is saved?" Or "I really hope he was saved before he died so that I know he is in heaven."

Many of you readers already know what this means, but bear with me. I have a thought-provoking story to share with you. See what you think!

But first, traditionally, salvation means that you have prayed to ask God to come into your life. Romans 10:9–10 says,

If you declare with your mouth, "Jesus is Lord" and believe in your heart that God raised Him from the dead, you will be saved. For it is with your heart that you believe and are justified, and it is with your mouth that you profess your faith and are saved.

Romans 10:13 adds, "For, 'Everyone who calls on the name of the Lord will be saved.'"

Here is the thought-provoking story. While this story is all true, there are many differing opinions from those who have heard this story. Feel free to let me know what you think. See the end of the book as to how to communicate with me.

I had been living with an unsaved man for fifteen years whom I dearly loved. I was not saved until the last two years of our relationship. "Joe" was leaving to go on a business trip to California. We were talking about God before he left.

"I am not even sure there is a God," said Joe.

"Well, if there is no God, what do you think happens to you when you die?" I asked.

"I don't really know," was Joe's response.

On the tip of my tongue I wanted to say, "Well, you better figure it out!"

But I pulled back and said nothing because one of his daughters was standing there listening to us. I didn't want to scare her by saying that. I didn't want her to fear that her dad was going to die soon. He left to go to California, and as he pulled out of our long driveway, I stood and watched him until he was out of sight. This was something I don't normally do.

Ten days later he died while still on his trip to California. I felt he was not saved when he died because of our conversation. In that ten-day period, no one that I knew he was meeting with in California would have prayed with him for his salvation.

During our phone conversations, not only had I not prayed with him for his salvation but the conversation we had before he left never came up again. Since we had talked salvation various times in the past and he knew my thoughts on it, if he had prayed the prayer to ask God into his life, I think he would have told me.

I now had a different understanding about the word *heartbroken*. I was totally devastated. Not only was he dead, but I would not see him in heaven. It was all I could do to get through the mechanics of life. Without the help of my family and time with God, I don't know how I would have done all that needed to be done.

It also made me wonder how people who do not have God in their lives do it. How do they find comfort and healing from such devastation without Him? Thankfully I didn't have to find that out.

There were two different ministers participating in his funeral. His family was Catholic, so I asked one of their priests to do part of the service. I wanted his daughters to experience whatever members of the Catholic church do for someone who has died. I also asked one of my sons, who was a youth pastor at the time, to do part of the service. While I knew that my son would talk about salvation at some point and he did, I wasn't sure what the priest would talk about.

To my surprise, the priest talked about salvation but in a way I had only heard one other time. He talked about the fact that he felt there were seconds before we completely die that we, while unconscious, can still be saved. He felt that during those few seconds, God comes to us and gives us one last chance to ask Him into our lives. The priest told us that we may not be able to judge if Joe was in heaven or not. But we should have hope that Joe, at the last minute, welcomed God into his life.

His theory gave me hope that Joe was in heaven. I didn't mull this idea over in my mind until several days after the funeral. As happens to all of us that lose loved ones, we can get lost in the duties required to take care of business for a while. But then, everyone goes home, the business is handled and there is time to think—time to grieve and heal.

As a nurse and from a medical standpoint, I remember being trained to use the defibrillator in the hospital. You know—that small machine that sends electrical impulses into the heart. On TV, you will hear the person using that machine yell "clear" first, to get everyone away from the patient so the electricity doesn't hurt them. Then the patient who is being fibrillated jumps, even though unconscious, as the electricity goes through his or her heart. Now they have portable units, automated external defibrillator, AED units, in a variety of places.

In that class, we were told that there were four minutes when someone is clinically dead, meaning they have stopped breathing and their heart has stopped. But during those four minutes, they still have enough oxygen in their bodies to possibly be brought back to life easier than after those four minutes.

The teacher stressed how important it is to get to patients within those four minutes to do CPR and defibrillate them. Just because we get to them within those four minutes does not mean everyone will live. It means if they can be resuscitated, that four minutes will be an advantage to bringing them back to life.

So as a nurse, I can agree with the priest's thoughts of last-minute salvation. I can also agree that Jesus can come and ask us if we want Him in our lives. John 14:2–3 states,

> My Father's house has many rooms; if that were not so, would I have told you that I am going there to prepare a place for you? And if I go and prepare a place for you, I *will come back and take you to*

be with me that you also may be where
I am.

I feel that says Jesus does spiritually return to us
in the last seconds to take us to heaven to be with
Him. It gives me peace, especially when I think of children dying. Jesus comes to children and takes them to
heaven. The child does not have to find the way alone.

That fear of dying we all have will be relieved by
the presence of Jesus. He is right there during our
final seconds to take us to heaven with Him. Once we
are saved, we are guaranteed to go to heaven. At some
point if someone asks you, "Do you think when you
die that you are going to heaven?" *Yes*, is the answer!

As a nurse, I have repeatedly seen the peace that
patients have before they die. I was not saved at the
time in my life that I was working as a nurse in the
hospital. Therefore, I never knew to question if any of
my patients were saved or not.

Another medical experience that I can look back
on and see God in the situation is when we did bring
patients back to life and they were not happy about
it. There were times, especially when I worked in ICU
and ER, that it was my responsibility to defibrillate a
patient who was dying. Most patients, after they regained consciousness, were happy to be alive.

However, there were some who were not happy that
we brought them back to life. I remember one very old,
very lovely, passive lady who was critical. She went
into cardiac arrest, and we went into action. After she
regained consciousness, she swore at us and was very
angry that we brought her back.

We asked her why she felt that way. She told us
there were two reasons. First, she had done what she

was most afraid to do, which was die. Second, she had gone to heaven and didn't want to leave there. She cried and continued to be very upset with us. This was before the time of being able to say that you do not want resuscitated. Back then, we resuscitated everyone.

I started to hear a lot about heaven from the patients we, did resuscitate. Many had the same story. They would talk about a bright light, seeing relatives or seeing God. They felt a peace, happiness, and joy that was unexplainable since they had never felt those emotions at that level while on earth.

There are a variety of books and articles about people who have experienced what these patients were talking about. I had heard these things before. But there is nothing like hearing it directly from someone who has experienced it.

The next part of my explanation will give pause to those who do not believe in visions or other ways that God uses to speak to us. There are times pictures pop into my brain that are as clear as watching a show on TV. At the same time, I get a nudge in my spirit, which tells me God is communicating with me through a vision in my head.

One day, a few months after Joe had died, I was sitting in a pew in church crying beyond any consolation that could have been offered—that is until a vision came into my mind. With my eyes closed and still crying, I saw Jesus standing on my right side and Joe standing on my left side and me sitting in that pew with my head in the hands. Immediately I felt peace, and I felt sure that Joe was in heaven with God. The vision only lasted seconds, but the peace has lingered forever in my spirit.

Later, as I collected myself, I wondered, "But how could Joe be in heaven? He wasn't even sure there was a God. When would he have prayed for his salvation in the ten days between seeing him and his death?" I have often asked those questions to myself and to others.

I feel the answer must be that God did spiritually come to Joe seconds before he died—that God had to have given him a last chance to allow Him to come into Joe's life. There is no other explanation.

More recently, as I have been with others as they are dying, I have been given another vision. Twice I have been at someone's bedside with my eyes closed, praying, I have seen in my head Jesus come as that person is experiencing his or her final breaths.

I know that there are many who don't believe in visions or hearing God tell us something in our heads, but I am not one of them. Having experienced both situations myself, I can only tell you what I have experienced as truthfully as I can explain it. I can only hope that by being truthful and by telling you humbly what I have experienced, that it gives you pause. This might give someone reason to go to prayer asking God into your life because I know that I know that I know that Joe is in heaven.

As it states in John 14:3, "And if I go and prepare a place for you, I will come back and take you to be with me that you also may be where I am." I felt like this was what I was seeing.

Again, traditionally, if you desire to become saved, someone will spend time with you and talk with you something like this or a variation of this.

They may start by asking you questions like: Do

you believe there is a God? Do you believe that Jesus died on the cross and was raised from the dead?

They may help you understand the salvation process by quoting you some scripture. An example would be Romans 10:9. "If you declare with your mouth, 'Jesus is Lord', and you believe in your heart that God raised him from the dead, you will be saved."

If you say yes, then they may ask you, "Would you be willing to repeat a prayer after me that will bring God into your life? That prayer will ensure you that you will go to heaven and spend eternity in God's kingdom."

If you say yes again, they will ask you to repeat after them a prayer something like this one:

Heavenly Father,

> I want you to be my Lord and come into my life. I believe Jesus died on the cross and was raised from the dead. Forgive me my sins. Help me to follow You for the rest of my life. I pray these things in Your name. Amen.

If you just prayed that prayer and meant what you prayed, you are now saved. If you did not read it with intent in your heart for it to be a prayer for your salvation, come back when you are ready and re-pray this prayer when you are sure that you truly want to do this.

That return time can be after you finish this book or months from now when you feel moved to pray it. Fold this page over when you are done reading it, or mark it in another way so you can come back to it.

If it is a library book or a friend's book that you

have borrowed, just rewrite the prayer and stick it somewhere where you can find it later.

If you did pray it and meant it, your next step is to get involved with a Bible-teaching church. But if you don't know which one that might be in your area, do as I did. I spent a summer going to different churches in my area and stayed at the one that I felt most moved to return to after my search was done. You will feel the Lord's presence at a church, but you may not realize what it is that you are feeling. You just know that it feels good there.

If you did pray that prayer and meant it, congratulations!

You now are a child of God too!

3

Your Own Story

Dear Reader,

Yes, I know you have a story too. And no, just because I was sexually abused, I don't think my story is a better one than yours. Nor do I feel that I am privileged or that I am owed anything because of my sexual abuse. I feel led to put some things in writing that might trigger someone to get help or do something to help themselves to a better life, which hopefully includes God.

If I hadn't experienced what I did as a child, I wouldn't be who I am today. I wouldn't be able to help the types of ladies that I am able to help. And my experience with satanic ritual abuse allows me to talk about a group of women who, up until now, were thought to be liars. It is a topic that you never talk about. Many don't believe it happens in real life.

Everyone has a story. That includes you. Even if your topic is the same topic as mine, in some way, your story is also different than mine. That doesn't mean that my story will help someone to be better or feel better and yours won't. It just means that something

I say may hit or trigger someone in a positive way because of the way I state it or that my experience reminds them of their experience in a different way than your story does.

Your experience and the way you tell it may hit or trigger someone that my story has not for whatever reason. Think about sharing your story too when you feel God is leading you to do so. You may be instrumental in helping someone heal or even save a life, in more than one way.

You don't have to be sexually abused or physically hurt in any way to have a story that God wants you to share with others. Your story may be just what they need to hear at that time no matter what the topic. You may feel it is too routine or not worth telling. That is because you have lived with that story for a long time. It may not feel dramatic enough or worthy enough in your mind.

If you feel like you have been nudged in some way to share, you need to share. Some of you may be led to write a book or do public speaking. Some of you will only tell your story to one other person in your whole lifetime. When God leads you to do so, in whatever form He leads you to do it, it will be the right story in the right form at the right time for the right person to hear. It will be every bit as important, and maybe more important, than my story written here.

What's the difference between a story and testimony? God and the truth. Nothing but the truth, the whole truth. (So, help me God!)

The Webster's dictionary defines a story as, "an account of imaginary or real people and events told for entertainment. A testimony is a formal written or spoken statement, especially one given in a court of law. A public recounting of a religious conversion or experience."

Stories can be embellished or changed to suit your own desires. Out and out lies may be put together to make us look important or special. When it becomes a testimony, you are swearing an oath to God to tell the truth to the best of your knowledge or remembrance.

Stories can be remembered differently by different people even though they lived through the same thing side by side. My brother and I got to spend a weekend together just the two of us. We started telling stories from our past. While we were in the same room, at the same time, living the same experience, we remembered it differently. Neither of us were making anything up. It's how that situation translated out for each of us.

We interpret things differently as men and women, child and adult, and our past experiences influence how we view things. But a testimony is your story as you remember you living through it and your idea of how it all came out in the end. It should be the truth as you know it.

For me, there are times when I interchange the words story and testimony as I verbally deliver something to someone. It is dependent on who I am speaking with at the time and what he or she is living through.

Some people might be at a place in their lives where the last thing they want now is a pushy Christian shoving God down their throat. At least, that's how it might feel to them. I might tell them some light story if nudged by God to do so. But these light stories lean toward a testimony. While I might not use His name, God is there in the story.

If I am speaking to a room of people who have come

to hear about God, I use the term *testimony*. Often, I have found that when I tell my testimony, while it is the truth and about God, I might only tell the beginning. Or I might only tell a middle portion of it, again as led by God. I have found God an excellent judge of what this person needs to hear from me now.

Many of us have long testimonies or many testimonies, particularly if we have been Christians for a long time. What to tell, who, and when can be confusing. I have learned to open my mouth and see what comes out, leaving the responsibility to God to pick and choose.

Not everyone who comes to me for counseling comes because he or she has been sexually abused. The story of my salvation experience may be more appropriate than my testimony about my sexual abuse. After a certain amount of sessions with them, if I may be sensing that God is going to reveal something about their past that they don't realize yet, I may add to my testimony.

TD Jakes, who is a bishop and TV pastor with a huge following, was telling a story one day on his show called the *Potter's Touch*. The story went something along these lines. He was talking with a new, young pastor who was also a PK, preacher's kid. Having been raised in the church and a graduate of a college with a pastoral degree program, this young pastor was champing at the bit to get a larger flock.

As the two of them chatted, TD Jakes noticed something. This young pastor seemed to not have a testimony. When TD asked him about it, the young pastor replied that he had none to give. The young pastor had had a great life, with great parents and no major trauma in his life.

TD asked him, "How can you identify with your parishioner who is sitting there telling you about the disaster they are experiencing now? How can you feel empathy, pain, or sorrow for them when you have not experienced it yourself?"

What an interesting thought. There are probably very few people out there who have not had at least one hard time in his or her life. You may think, *How can I complain when my experience of pain was so minor compared to someone else's pain?*

The answer to that question is there is still someone out there who needs to hear your testimony. If God is nagging you to write down what has happened to you, or your family or a friend of yours, He is preparing you to use that information at some point in your life.

You may write it and stick it in a drawer for twenty years. Or you may write a book or an article one day. But the bottom line is, if He is asking you to do something with your story, you need to obey.

One of my clients has had MS for twenty-one years. The last several years she has been practically wheelchair bound. I have been in Bible studies with her as well as recently becoming her counselor. She is dealing with two hard things. One is the need to transition into a retirement setting. And second, suddenly, God is preparing her to share her testimony and her relationship with Him with others.

She has always wanted to affect others for God's kingdom but wondered what she could offer. Living in a house alone and being unable to ambulate well, she has had fewer people relationships and interactions in her life. What could someone with limited mobility, limited experiences, and a limited relationship with God do?

God started to direct her into how to get a closer relationship with Him. She needed to spend more time with Him, which she was doing. Then He started to show her how she could become a prayer warrior and affect others in that manner. As this all transpired, she began to find herself praying for someone who she thought just happened to come up in her spirit. Before long, that person would somehow come into closer contact with her through a visit, a phone call, or an accidental meeting.

Now God was showing her ways she would influence not only the people she loved but those she would meet in her retirement situation. There would be those who she could read the Bible to, read the cards they receive in the mail to them, or just visit and pray with them. She had a motorized wheelchair and could get around to others who were even more limited in their mobility than she was.

As traumatic as this move from her house to a retirement village would be for her, this was going to open a whole new ministry for her. Slowly God was helping her to accept the move and see it in a positive light instead of as a negative situation.

What has God been nagging you to do or change in your life? How has He been asking you to step out of the boat or out of your box and do something? What thought or action have you been too scared to try or even think about? Is there a thought that keeps coming back around to you in various ways telling you the same thing again and again? What idea keeps coming in and out of your thoughts and you tell yourself it's all in your head? You think you are making this up!

We are all here for a purpose! God has a variety of ways to communicate with us about that purpose. It is unnerving to think about making that jump into something that will stretch us beyond our comfort zone.

But let me reassure you that the leap of faith is worth is. When you work hard for God's kingdom, He works hard for you in your kingdom. You will see things that tell you that you have found favor in Christ. Prime parking places become available just when you enter the parking lot. Situations that could be challenging become situations that you sail through with victory.

I had a small fender bender in the middle of a pouring down rain. The person with me needed to see God's favor for some reason. This situation became a way for her to see it. She was flustered and anxious for me because of my dented fender. I was at peace. When I reviewed the day with her, I could show her all the positive things that happened.

The downpour stopped just as I needed to exit my car to see what damage was done. No one was hurt. My car was drivable, and I was very close to the garage I go to for service on my car. We drove right there even though it was in Friday, late-afternoon traffic. There were only a few people there, so a technician came over to me as I pulled in. He told me they did not do that type of repair but an arm of their corporation did. That garage was right down the street.

I pulled in there and got immediate service. Not only was the service immediate, but they had a relationship with the company that I had my insurance with for my car. They could hook up computers and see what type of coverage I had. Within fifteen or twenty minutes, I was out of there with an estimate and an appointment on Monday for the repair and was on my way to finish shopping.

God's favor was all over that situation. I do not believe in coincidence or luck. God is the master of multitasking, and He controls the reason all that happened at the time it did and with the person I had with me in my car that day.

I firmly believe that fender bender was for her purpose. He has been working on her for a while, and this was part of her training. She needed to observe Him at work in someone's life in a way that was easy for her to see. She needed to find God's peace in action. Her life is far from peaceful right now. I am hoping that changes soon.

Stepping out in God's purpose starts with your testimony. Life as God's ambassador will evolve from that. He will move you from place to place and purpose to purpose. Your purpose will change over time with no effort on your part to keep searching.

Will you still have bad days? Sure. Will you find times you are doing something that brings fear to your spirit? Yes, but you will learn to deal with it and turn it around. Will you experience a joy, freedom, and peace that are beyond what you are used to living with now?

Absolutely!

4

That's a Wrap!

It's time to end this book. What an experience for me! I have had an article or two and a poem published, but I have never written a book before. I suspect some of you avid readers who are used to reading books by well-known authors can tell this is my first, and as far as I know now, my last.

When it came time to sign on with a publisher, I became anxious about how I was going to accomplish all this. Would I really be able to do it? Had I picked the right publisher? Was this really going to happen? But as God tends to do for me, He pointed out a different perspective when I went off in a wrong direction.

As I mentioned before, I am a retired RN. While I worked various places and units, my favorite was ICU and ER. I loved the adrenaline rush of a cardiac arrest or a major car accident. I was sorry others were hurting, but for me, I would kick into professional gear and do what was needed. I had no trouble defibrillating patients. I had no trouble with a patient who was hemorrhaging. The challenge of handling the crisis was the focus.

Working these units was like my tennis game. I was always better at the net. If I must stand and think about things, I go too far or overthink. If I can react on instinct and my gut, I do much better. Do I use my forehand or backhand on this ball? Too much thinking!

If I compare working with a publisher to working on a dying patient as far as stress level, why was I anxious? As a nurse, I had the life of a person in my hands. Life-and-death decisions were a norm for me. If I made a mistake, it could cost someone their life.

No one was going to die because of my decision to write this book. If I had the wrong publisher, unlike giving the wrong blood type to the wrong patient, no one would have an adverse reaction but me. And that reaction would be far from life threatening.

This helped me to question, why would this decision to publish a book cause me to become anxious for any reason? Because it was something I had never done before. God had asked me to step out of my comfort zone. So, buck up and move on, Darci.

Perspective. It all has to do with perspective. What is the worst that can happen working with a publisher? What was the worst that could happen working on a critical patient? I survived the ER and ICU, and so did most of my patients. I would survive this too. (I will leave it up to the publisher as to if they survive working with me!)

Let's look at perspective for a short time here. Perspective is defined as a particular attitude toward or way of regarding something—a point of view.

This is something God must work on with me frequently. I find it is something I need to work on often with my clients too. Perspective works hand and hand with expectation. We set an expectation in our minds about how something is supposed to happen or work out. When it does not work out to our expectation, we are hurt.

We get married and expect out marriage to be a certain way. It does not work out that way, and we get hurt, depressed, and angry. Yet if we compare what it was like living single or what it is like living with in a marriage that is far worse than ours, what does that show us? At times, it helps us to put things in perspective. Often that helps us cope or find peace living with where we are. At times, it doesn't help.

Sometimes we live in a situation that repeatedly hurts us or is not what we thought it would be. Would it help us to change our expectations? Can we look at this from another perspective? How can we deal with this situation to make it better?

If we have tried our best to improve it and change the situation to meet our expectation and it continuously does not meet that expectation, we need to be the one to make the change. We are the only thing we can control in the situation. We cannot control others, no matter how hard we try. The only sure thing we can change is our own perspective and expectations.

I need a new perspective. I need to change my expectations of that person who continuously hurts me. My present expectation for that person is something he or she may never achieve. But if I lower or change my expectations for that person and set ones that I know he or she can achieve, I will get hurt less often.

I know he is never going to remember to put the seat down on the toilet. It's been five years of nagging and it has not changed. So, I change my habit of going in to the bathroom already angry knowing the seat is up. My change is that I form a new habit to meet what is occurring.

I always lower the seat before I start to prepare my clothing for that deed. Things that become habit often are done with no forethought once learned. I do it over and over again and remain at peace about it.

If he does remember by chance, it's a good day and I feel good. If he doesn't remember, I no longer get angry every time I go to the bathroom, because my new habit has become automatic. I don't think about the toilet seat any more. Plus, I don't sit down without thinking and get wet. I always have a seat to sit on, and life can keep moving in a positive flow.

Whole books have been written about the topics of expectation, perspective, and how to live with a difficult person or situation. I only want to mention these topics here because they are important. They are something you can change or do to take care of some hurt you may be experiencing. This is something common to many people. Those who make these changes have a better life. Those who decide to continue with the anger, hurt, and unforgiveness get bitter.

So often I have had women come to me about their marriages. Things are not going well. How can they change their husband? We do look at the situation as it is with God and take His advice. There are some changes we can make within ourselves no matter the situation.

Once we have identified and worked on what God wants us to do within ourselves, the bottom line is that only God can change your husband. But you and God can work on your perspective and your expectations to change the situation to make it tolerable for both of you.

It is hard work. It does take effort on your part to change. You will fall back into your old habit at least once or say, "Why should I change? He's the one ..." Because God is asking you to be the one, at least this time. But with time and effort, patience and forgiveness, you will be successful.

Speaking of forgiveness, I want to talk about forgiveness and bitterness. Again, there are two words that God needs to help many of us with often. I have seen the harm the enemy does to people who aren't able to forgive a situation and bitterness takes over.

Also, again, there are whole books written about these topics. My objective is to remind you about these emotions. I have heard a variety of pastors preach on emotions and how we let them control our lives. They also preach on how to take control of our emotions.

Emotions are an area that the enemy loves. This is a place we frequently leave open for him to come in. "I refuse to forgive her. You don't understand what she did to me. I don't care what God says I should do, I will never forgive her."

A surprise that many of my ladies find out about when they come to me is that forgiving ourselves is often harder than forgiving others. We think we have forgiven them, but deep down we may not have. We don't think of forgiving ourselves as part of that deal.

No matter how wrong that person may have been to do what he or she did to you, you still had some influence in how the situation was handled. Often unknowingly, until we look at the situation through God's eyes, we have contributed to the issue in some negative manner. Through God's eyes, He will show us our contribution. Sometimes it takes more than one try to forgive ourselves because we take on the guilt the enemy repeatedly reminds us of in our minds. "You call yourself a good Christian and you act like that?"

The enemy is so good at pulling us down on ourselves. And we are so good at receiving that condemnation. It doesn't take much to hang on to the negative. Add a little stubbornness on our part to the mix, which keeps us from giving in to forgiving, and the enemy is celebrating our return to his kingdom.

But because we are working hard for God's kingdom, and we know He always wins, we are able with His help to get our minds and spirits in the right place. The story of David and Bathsheba in 2 Samuel 11–12 is a perfect example. It took Nathan, a person outside of the situation, to get David to see what he had done. David's stubbornness kept him from righting the wrong for a long time. But he did it. And we can too when it is our turn.

When we let unforgiveness slip even further down into bitterness, we create a whole new depth of pain for ourselves and the situation. Bitterness becomes a poison in our blood stream that is not cured by the normal antibiotics of life. Surgery, performed by the Great Physician, needs to be added to the mix to heal the disease process.

The enemy has invaded the surrounding tissue and organs along with the blood flow. Antibiotics alone will not do the trick. Dr. Lord needs to cut out the decaying tissue and area of the organs involved to rid the body of the invasion. Our Surgeon is always good at His profession and always successful.

If unforgiveness is taken care of in the early stages of the disease process, God's antibiotics will do the job. Surgery can be avoided along with the additional pain and suffering involved with the added invasion of bitterness. Either way, though, the Lord will win if we choose to get back on His team.

Forgiving God is another tough one. We blame God for the mess we are experiencing. And sometimes He has allowed the mess to occur for His own reason. But blaming Him can be tricky. We add guilt and shame to the mix because we feel it is wrong to have those feelings about our Lord.

I have told more than one client that God is a big boy. He can handle your anger and rage. You might as well tell Him exactly how you feel because He knows it anyway. Get it all out. Then ask His forgiveness for your reaction, for help with the forgiveness you need to do toward others, yourself, and Him, and for protection from the enemy while you are working on this process. It's not an easy or quick process.

More times than I care to admit, God has had to say the same thing to me during one of my life's hiccups. I will be acting just like the clients I have tried to help in a situation. God will say to me, "Now, what would you be telling one of your ladies in this situation?" The teacher, *me*, needs to take some of her own medicine at times!

However, having to do this myself has helped me to encourage my ladies. While they will have times when they are not as successful as they hoped to be in the process, we all go there. Ask God what you were supposed to learn out of what just happened, and then seek forgiveness. Shove the enemy out of your brain when he tries to make you feel guilty and move on. Try again.

Another issue frequently addressed when our lives are off kilter is rejection. Every one of us has been rejected by someone in our lives. It can be a friend, a loved one, or a group of people. That rejection not only hurts but hangs on for a long time.

Because of the pain and the length of its endurance, we build walls and ways of handling life that add additional pain instead of helping. Our reaction to that rejection sets us up for the rest of our lives, until we deal with it and react to the world in an unhealthy way.

We become so used to the heaviness we carry from that rejection that we no longer realize we are reacting to it anymore. We forget all about it and go about living. But our way of living is unhealthy. And if we work with others, raise our children, or just want others to see Christ in us, we may be failing in those relationships, not knowing why things are not working out for the best.

Again, God has all the answers. Do we allow time for Him to help us with those things? Do we obey what He is asking us to do? Or are we saying, "This stuff is nuts. It's all in my head. I don't want to deal with this," and go eat a hot fudge sundae to make it all go away?

As Jeremiah 29:11 says, God has a great plan for our lives. Well, so does the enemy have a plan for our lives, but not such a good one. The enemy wants to ruin our marriages, our homes, our ministries. He wants us miserable, bitter, suffering, and fallen.

The way to ruin the enemy's life is to get more and more into the plans God has for you. How do you know what those plans are? Get into the will of God and you will succeed. To find out the will of God and how to follow that plan of action in your life is to spend more time with God.

Learn how to hear God in your life. Learn how to

figure out when you are going left when God told you
to go right. Believe that when you fail in your mind,
you have not failed in God's mind. The only way you
can fail is to not try. If you are trying, God will say,
"*Again*. Try that *again*! You'll do better next time."

Learn how to spend time with God being quiet.
We can all pray. It's hard not to pray when you are
spending time with God. But when we are praying, we
can't always hear what He is saying to us. It's hard to
be quiet and listen to what is in your head. It's hard
to know if what's in your head is from God or you. It's
all from God. He is in you.

The Holy Spirit is already living in you. He is filling
your head and spirit with ideas all the time. We are
the one that overrule him. We are the one who says,
"I don't want to do that. An example of this is the rich
man in Matthew 19:16–24. Jesus told him how to get
eternal life, and the rich man was the one who refused
to comply. The rich man would not give up his riches.

The more time you spend in God's world, the less
time you will spend in Satan's world. You can't be fulfilling God's plan and Satan's plan at the same time.
At times, we can slip from one world in to the other.
But there is always a way to get back into the plan that
is victorious in the end.

Another hot topic for women is how to be a submissive wife and not lose your identity. As Christian
women, we want to honor God's direction. And God
does let us know His thoughts through scripture
(Ephesians 5:21–33). Out of reverence for Christ, we
are asked to "submit to our husbands as to the Lord."
Many of my ladies who come for counseling are having
an issue with this.

Jesus also talks about how the husband is to love

his wife as Christ loves His church. He gave His life for the church. And they are to love their wives as they do their own bodies. Would your husband give his life for you? Some of you will be able to say yes immediately. Others not so much! God honors man only if he honors his wife. If he does not honor his wife, a man may not receive blessings from God in return. In the New Living Translation, 1 Peter 3:7 says: "In the same way, you husbands must give honor to your wives. Treat your wife with understanding as you live together." She may be weaker than you are, but she is your equal partner in God's gift of new life. Treat her as you should so your prayers will not be hindered.

This marriage relationship is a two-sided coin and is to be honored by both. If you are married to a great Christian man, this is an easier person to submit to as asked to do. But what if your husband is not on his best Christian behavior? Are we required to honor that man as well? Is there a difference between honor and submit?

Submit means accept or yield to a superior force or to the authority or will of another person. Honor means regard with great respect, fulfill (an obligation) or keep (an agreement).

In the marriages, I have observed that work well from a Christianity standpoint, there are times when to submit is appropriate and times when to honor is appropriate. Whether it is the man or the woman, we all slip in and out of our level of obedience to God. Sometimes we are doing well. Other times we are struggling to be at our best.

Because we may not be at our best, it does not mean we will stay there forever. When we get it back to-gether, then it is appropriate to go back to submission.

However, the husbands I see who are strong heads of the family are all doing the same thing when it comes to submission.

If both the husband and the wife are not in agreement, whatever they are discussing does not get done. If the husband wants to buy a new car and the wife is not in agreement after praying about it, they wait and look at this idea another time. The key also is the wife's answer is after a time of prayer, not just from her own thoughts.

Both the husband and wife seek God in all things. That doesn't mean they don't have bad days in their marriage. It means God is involved in the bad days as well as the good.

We are to love and care for others. Putting God is first, and pleasing each other should be next in line. If I work hard to do what is right and proper for my husband, hopefully he will see that. And if he hasn't figured it out ahead of me, hopefully he will want to do the same for me.

Another thing to consider is how you pick your husband. What do you look for in a man? And what should you bring to the table of marriage?

In an author unknown article in one of my local free newspapers, these questions are answered. It is written from a self-sufficient woman's perspective. Since she can pay her own bills and conduct her own life without a man, what does she look for a man to do?

She writes: "I am looking for a man who is striving for excellence in every aspect of life." She includes excellence in: conversation and mental stimulation, spiritually so not to be "unevenly yoked," financially, understanding "who will keep me grounded," integrity, family-oriented "head of the household," and respect, which is to work both ways.

She goes on to say, "I will find it much easier to be submissive to a man who is taking care of his business. I have no problem being submissive ... I just want him to be worthy. God made woman to be a helpmate for man. I can't help a man if he can't help himself."

She states that she is not asking any more than she is asking of herself and that she will be striving for excellence at the same time. "The writer of Proverbs says, 'who can find a virtuous woman? For her price is far above rubies' (Proverbs 31:10)." When talking about women of the Bible and that we are today's women of the Bible, we must look at Proverbs 31. If you are unfamiliar with this Proverb, in your own timing, no matter if you are male or female, it would behoove you to take time to read all of Proverbs 31.

Here are ways you can contact me:

- www.youaretodayswomenofthebible.com
- Email address: Darcijeffries@yahoo.com
- Facebook: Darci Jeffries

David Jeremiah through his ministry Turning Point said, "Satan tests us at our weakness, so that he might destroy us; God tests us at our strengths, so that He might employ us."

May the Lord bless you and use you to your full capacity for His kingdom. May you find the *you* He created you to be and share *you* with the rest of us. I wish you peace, joy, freedom, and a life full of the Father, Son, and Holy Spirit!

Bibliography

Jeremiah, David. *Turning Point Magazine and Devotional*. San Diego, CA: Turning Point Ministry, 2015 & 2017

Meyer, Joyce. *Battlefield of the Mind*. Fenton, MO: Warner Faith Publisher, 2002

Moore, Beth, *Beloved Disciple,* Nashville, TN, Lifeway Church Resources, 2002.